"Bet[s]... about parenting. It is a book by a mom that brings insight and passion to life's most important job: raising children. I highly recommend it."

—William J. Bennett,
author of *The Book of Virtues*

"*It Takes a Parent* is so important to t[he]... [nex]t generation of children that I intend [to...] [a]ll the parents and prospective parents i[n...]

—Dr. [...]er,
author of *The Proper Care and Feeding of Husbands*
and *Stupid Things Parents Do to Mess Up Their Kids*

"This book is an important, no-nonsense, and often hilarious account of parenting in a culture gone wild. Whether you are a parent or would-be parent, or you know parents who need help, Betsy Hart's book is an essential resource." —Laura Ingraham,
host of the nationally syndicated *Laura Ingraham Show*
and author of *Shut Up and Sing*

"Brimming with wisdom and common sense, *It Takes a Parent* gently but decisively demolishes the modern laissez-faire approach to parenting. The village can't do it. The 'parenting culture' is too wimpy. It takes a parent, preferably one tutored by Betsy Hart's excellent book."

—Mona Charen,
syndicated newspaper columnist and author of *Do-Gooders*

continued . . .

"Could you use the insights of a wise and witty mother who cares as much as you do about raising happy, well-behaved children with strong character and a lively faith? Meet Betsy Hart. Spend your children's allowance on this book—it's for them." —Kate O'Beirne,
Washington editor, *National Review*

"Practical, straight-shooting, supportive advice for parents. You will be glad you read this book." —Robert Shaw, M.D.,
director, The Family Institute of Berkeley,
and author of *The Epidemic*

"As a marriage and family counselor and parent of three teenagers, I appreciate Betsy Hart's straightforward approach, which empowers me, the parent. Her critique of today's parenting culture and her emphasis on reaching the heart of your children make this a great read for any parent." —Dr. Paul Randolph,
counselor, Christian Counseling and Educational Foundation,
and adjunct professor, Biblical Theological Seminary

"It takes a bold, wise, and compassionate author like Betsy Hart to give today's parents the advice they so badly crave." —Danielle Crittenden,
author of *What Our Mothers Didn't Tell Us:*
Why Happiness Eludes the Modern Woman

It Takes a Parent

How the Culture of

Pushover Parenting Is

Hurting Our Kids—and

What to Do About It

Betsy Hart

A Perigee Book

THE BERKLEY PUBLISHING GROUP
Published by the Penguin Group
Penguin Group (USA) Inc.
375 Hudson Street, New York, New York 10014, USA
Penguin Group (Canada), 90 Eglinton Avenue East, Suite 700, Toronto, Ontario M4P 2Y3, Canada
(a division of Pearson Penguin Canada Inc.)
Penguin Books Ltd., 80 Strand, London WC2R 0RL, England
Penguin Group Ireland, 25 St. Stephen's Green, Dublin 2, Ireland (a division of Penguin Books Ltd.)
Penguin Group (Australia), 250 Camberwell Road, Camberwell, Victoria 3124, Australia
(a division of Pearson Australia Group Pty. Ltd.)
Penguin Books India Pvt. Ltd., 11 Community Centre, Panchsheel Park, New Delhi—110 017, India
Penguin Group (NZ), Cnr. Airborne and Rosedale Roads, Albany, Auckland 1310, New Zealand
(a division of Pearson New Zealand Ltd.)
Penguin Books (South Africa) (Pty.) Ltd., 24 Sturdee Avenue, Rosebank, Johannesburg 2196,
South Africa

Penguin Books Ltd., Registered Offices: 80 Strand, London WC2R 0RL, England

While the author has made every effort to provide accurate telephone numbers and Internet addresses at
the time of publication, neither the publisher nor the author assumes any responsibility for errors, or for
changes that occur after publication. Further, publisher does not have any control over and does not
assume any responsibility for author or third-party websites or their content.

PRINTING HISTORY
G. P. Putnam's Sons hardcover edition / August 2005
Perigee trade paperback edition / August 2006

Perigee trade paperback ISBN: 0-399-53261-7

The Library of Congress has cataloged the G. P. Putnam's Sons hardcover edition as follows:

Hart, Betsy (Betsy Canfield)
    It takes a parent : how the culture of pushover parenting is hurting our kids—and what to do about it /
Betsy Hart.
      p.   cm.
    Includes bibliographical references and index.
    ISBN 0-399-15303-9
    1. Parenting—United States.   2. Parent and child—United States.   3. Child rearing—United States.
I. Title.
HQ755.8.H376   2005   2005046432
306.874'0973—dc22

PRINTED IN THE UNITED STATES OF AMERICA

10   9   8   7   6   5   4   3   2   1

Most Perigee Books are available at special quantity discounts for bulk purchases for sales promotions,
premiums, fund-raising, or educational use. Special books, or book excerpts, can also be created to fit
specific needs. For details, write: Special Markets, The Berkley Publishing Group, 375 Hudson Street,
New York, New York 10014.

For Peter, Victoria, Madeleine, and Olivia

Because they are the lights of my life—
and because they will forever have to bear the burden of
having a mother who wrote a book on parenting

Acknowledgments

I feel a little funny writing acknowledgments for this book, not because there aren't wonderful people who made the project happen, but because it seems, well, a little self-congratulatory. I mean, what if in spite of the help I received from so many terrific people, I still can't write a book that folks outside my immediate family actually want to read?

But I've decided to take my chances with acknowledgments, anyway, because I see writing this book as sort of an "Are you kidding me?" moment in my life: I was given an incredible privilege to publicly address a matter about which I'm passionate. Even if it turns out that even my immediate family members don't each buy a copy (and they had darn well better), I will still, and always, look at writing this book as an extraordinary privilege—and that's the context in which I want to thank the many dear people who have given me the thrill of a lifetime.

At the top of the list has to be my agent, Teresa Hartnett, who convinced me that people outside my immediate family actually *would* buy *It Takes a Parent,* and without whose support and enthusiasm and incredibly valuable input the book just wouldn't have happened. I'm also so very grateful to my first editor at Putnam, Sheila Curry Oakes, who believed in the project and officially made me an author; to her successor, Marian Lizzi, who helped the book to blossom; and to Putnam senior editor John Duff, who so consistently encouraged me throughout the process.

Of course, I'm forever indebted to my editors at the Scripps Howard News Service — Washington, D.C., bureau chief Peter Copeland, Jay Ambrose (now retired), and Walter Veazey. Week after week they actually pay me to tell people what I think about things, which seemed always to amaze my mother in particular.

And then there are the many friends who offered valuable input on the book, who found ways with incredible aplomb to say, "You really, um, need to fix this," or who simply encouraged me, people like Jeanne Allen, Steve Huntley, and Melinda Sidak, to whom I am truly appreciative. And here I have to thank my dear friend Maria McCarthy, who gave me the biggest (undeserved) shot in the arm I could have asked for: When I called to tell her I was writing a book, she said, "Well, I just hope it's on parenting!"

Of course, there are the many wonderful friends and parents from whom I learned so very much, and who should have written this book instead of me, but for some reason God gave me the privilege of putting their demonstrably wise words into my own clumsy ones: people like Dave and Jennie Coffin, Paul and Brenda McNulty, Wes and Martha Wilson, March and Mariam Bell, and so many others who taught and encouraged me. Thank you from the bottom of my heart.

It will, I'm afraid, soon become clear to any reader of this book that much of it was written during the darkest and most difficult period of my life. Every friend listed above was great and steadfast help to me during that time — the Coffins stand out as people whose care and wisdom was particularly lucid, even at one o'clock in the morning.

But there were many other friends, too, whose love and affection and support and prayers allowed me to complete the book, and who helped me to find real joy and satisfaction in doing so. I am thankful for them all. Just a few of them are Helene Brenner, Lynne Carlson, and Marjorie Dannenfelser, who *always* had the right things to say; Trish Ryan, who was a beloved and trusted babysitter to my children and a friend to me; and Steve and Adrianne Schneider (and their adorable boys), who were the best next-door neighbors anybody ever had, and who were like second parents, and their sons like brothers, to my own children.

And then I moved with my kids back "home" to the Chicago area, and into a wonderful little town with people who have very big hearts and who welcomed us all—and I'm so grateful to those new friends, too.

And *almost* most of all, I'm profoundly thankful for my wonderful family: my dear father, who at eighty, when so many other people are confined to nursing homes, instead does things like take downhill skiing lessons and makes me look at the fabric samples he's considering for the furniture in his new high-rise apartment; my incredible mom, my dear friend who died way too young in 1995, and whose fierce and positive spirit has stayed with me (and my kids!) and strengthened me always; and my sister, Beverly Hayes, and my brothers, Dwight, David, and Dennis Canfield (and their families), whose incredible love, support, care, and concern for my children and me during such a hard time in our lives has proved to me that, well, you really *can* go home again.

But *most* of all, I want to thank the most precious people in my life: Peter, Victoria, Madeleine, and Olivia, because they have given me the courage and the hope to keep going and have caused me to find joy in doing so; because they have borne so much and borne it so well; and because they know me better than anyone else in the whole world—and they love me anyway.

Contents

Introduction

In a recent commercial for laundry detergent, a single mother of two teenagers is headed out on a date. She spills ketchup on herself while giving the kids dinner—Tide to the rescue. Later, as she's being dropped off by her fellow, she catches sight of her daughter in the house. Mom thinks to herself, I wonder if it's okay to kiss on the first date? Hmmm. I guess I'll ask my daughter.

Why? Because the daughter is wiser than her mom?

One popular parenting website, partnershipforchildren.com, tells parents that even if they *know* their child is lying, they shouldn't accuse the little one of any wrongdoing. They should instead talk with him about how "special" the truth is. They should tell him how proud they are when he tells the truth. And then they should just let that little conscience go to work.

But what if all the little conscience says is, "Great—I got away with it"?

Family therapist Ed Wimberly wants us parents to regularly ask ourselves whether we are giving our children *as many choices in life as possible*. The response is clearly supposed to be, "You bet I am!" He also tells us in his popular book *A Parent's Guide to Raising Great Kids* that "our kids deserve to feel good about themselves simply because they are, simply because they exist."

That's the message on kidshealth.org, too, in its section for children, which tells kids that "*it's the most important thing you have*. It's self-esteem!" (emphasis added). Meanwhile, the folks over at parentcenter .babycenter.com instruct parents to always accept their child's emotions and feelings "without judgment." And, of course, today whenever we see a child misbehave, what does the embarrassed parent almost always offer as an explanation? "He's just really tired!"

Welcome to the "parenting culture," a culture in which parents are essentially encouraged to idolize their children, to marvel at their inherent wisdom and goodness . . . and that's just for starters.

I know all about the parenting culture, because I have four little ones myself. As I write they are Peter, ten; Victoria, eight; Madeleine, five; and Olivia, three. And I know that it's thanks to the parenting culture that so many mothers and fathers believe they must make sure the kids *always* feel really special and really terrific about themselves—even when they are behaving terrifically badly. Of course, today kids don't behave badly—they just become exhausted.

The modern mom and dad are terrified of overlooking a "need" or bruising a delicate psyche. And heaven forbid our kids should ever suffer disappointment, irritation, or frustration.

We give our children choices whenever possible, and—good grief!—we search for alternatives to saying no. We don't want little ears to hear, "The answer is no, because I said so" from a parent. Self-esteem has replaced self-restraint or any ideas about esteeming others in the great pantheon of children's virtues. Agonizing with children about their all-important feelings has replaced the "Don't bother me now unless you're bleeding" refrain many of us heard as kids.

In fact such comments as "Don't interrupt, dear, I'm talking to Mr. Schneider" or "Go play, kids—the adults are talking," or "I can't focus on you now, honey, I'm on the phone—you'll have to wait till I'm off" are missing in far too many modern homes. That's because today's moms and dads are, essentially, encouraged to have their lives revolve around their children and to be willing to drop everything and anything to attend to them.

And spanking? Because of the parenting culture, the word is barely mentioned in polite society.

Many of our own parents would have thought these ideas were sort of silly. Our moms and dads weren't perfect, of course, and they had their own parenting fads to contend with. But few people I know would argue that today's kids are better off as a generation for all the over-wrought parenting the experts dictate to the modern parent. Nor do I think today's parents are any happier for all the expert advice. We're certainly not calmer. How can we be? Too many of us are too busy obsessing about *everything* having to do with junior.

The parenting culture is seductive and, of course, so are our kids! I've fallen into many of the parenting culture's traps myself. But I'm always saddened when I see parents who so consistently follow the par-enting culture's dictates that they are completely stressed out by their young children—even just one or two healthy ones—to the point where what should be a general delight and one of life's greatest joys has turned into "Just get me through these years!" (It makes sense that often the kids seem pretty miserable, too.)

Unfortunately, these parents will probably be saying the same thing when the teenage years hit. They love their kids like crazy, we all do, but their approach to life with their children has them constantly asking the question, "Are we having fun yet?"

A hundred years ago, the twentieth century was named the "Century of the Child" by Ellen Key, an early child advocate who wrote a book with that title in 1900. But the past hundred years might better have been called the "Century of the Child Expert."

It's that expertise on child rearing, the body of accepted dogma from "on high" about how children must be raised, that I call the "parenting culture." I'll look at that culture throughout this book. Sure, it's not exactly a monolith, but I'll show that the various strains of the parenting culture sure do seem to have been given the same general marching orders.

But are they going in the right direction?

In the twentieth century child rearing—which had been going on successfully for more than a few generations—was raised to a science. But the scientists had wildly contradictory ideas and often contradicted themselves as well. So, it's really no surprise that today few people would argue that the "science" of child rearing has gotten us very far after all.

I do not encourage parents to dismiss the advice of experts out of hand. I certainly agree that wisdom and knowledge can be found there. But I do encourage parents to climb out of the parenting culture's box—to recognize that *they* are the parents and they really do know what's best for their children. If parents can use any of the experts' advice to better meet their own parenting goals, that's great. But if they're intimidated by the experts or shirking their responsibilities as parents, they're doing themselves and their children a disservice.

Ten years ago, shortly after the birth of my first child, I started writing a weekly column for the Scripps Howard News Service. At first the column tended to focus on political and national issues, but over time, as my other babies came into the world, I began to turn the focus more to the culture, to children, and to parenting.

The response was amazing. If I wrote a column on a presidential campaign, I might get several dozen e-mails. But if I wrote a column saying, "Hey, who says we have to give children so many choices?" I might get more than one hundred positive responses. It seems that the culture in which we're raising our children—which includes the culture of the home—is what matters most to so many people. That became true for me and was reflected more and more in my writing.

I am no parenting expert in any traditional sense. I'm just a mom of four young kids, and every day I'm bombarded by what the parenting culture tells me I have to do to make my kids smarter, happier, more compliant, nicer, kinder—just generally *better*.

But to me, the parenting culture seems pretty self-obsessed, maybe a little too focused not just on having nearly perfect kids, but on being nearly perfect parents.

Sometimes I think the parenting culture just needs to lighten up.

Over and over again I found that the advice from the parenting culture—the magazines, books, television programs, and so on—didn't make sense. *Never* spank? *Always* build their self-esteem? Separate the bad behavior from the child? Feelings are always right? A lot of it didn't add up for me.

Fortunately, I've had many wise and good parents to turn to for advice, people who are confidently raising their kids or who have already done so. They've repeatedly given me good counsel—and it is often very different from that offered by the parenting culture.

And people in my own life have told me that I seem to be raising my children differently—they don't interrupt quite so much, or seem to throw tantrums whenever they are told "no," they don't appear to be the center of the family universe. When people come over for dinner, for instance, I can actually tell my kids to go play away from the "grown-up zone" while the adults are talking.

And my children seem to be surviving it all quite nicely.

Of course, sometimes I think, If you could only see what happens when you leave! My kids are kids—they bicker, they fight, they complain, they delight in annoying one another. My children have their own personalities and present their own challenges. One of them came into the world not wanting to ever cause anyone any problems; another is, I'm convinced, loosely affiliated with the Sopranos.

More than once I've said to my children in a resigned voice—as they fought tooth and nail over something as important as who would get the first scoops out of the new peanut butter jar—"Apparently, it's too late for me when it comes to parenting. Now I'm just hoping my book can help other moms and dads." (My kids have asked me to *please* stop saying that.)

Still, I confess, I do feel confident about parenting. Not because I have all the right answers, by any means, but because I know one thing: I am the mom. I know better than my kids, I love them more than anybody else in the world, and they benefit immensely from my being a confident parent. As a good friend said to my husband, Ben, and me before we started having children, "Decide early who will run your home—if it isn't you, it'll be the kids."

Statements like that make the parenting culture very nervous.

But there's so much more to parenting than who's in charge. Over time, wise parents have helped me see that parenting isn't just about getting the behavior right at the moment. It isn't just about stopping the tantrums or the backtalk, encouraging good manners or good sibling relations.

The real issue is getting to the hearts of my children. As a parent, I have to understand that their hearts are in danger, not just because of the world they live in, but because of the nature of children themselves. One hardly has to be a religious person to agree with the writer of Proverbs who said, "Folly is bound up in the heart of a child" (Proverbs 22:15). A child's heart is often trusting and loving, but it's also self-oriented and foolish, and such a danger to a child. I'll look at this more in chapter 7, "Misbehavior and Other Matters of the Heart."

When I say "heart," I mean more than just character. I suppose a child with good character might not lie, for instance, because he knows it's wrong. That's a fine thing, and it's an area in which we need to train our kids. But a child with a rightly oriented heart is growing toward genuinely disdaining lying and loving truth.

A child with good character might be nice to others because she knows politeness is appropriate. That's great. But a child with a rightly oriented heart is growing toward truly valuing, caring about, and respecting others, and so wanting them to know they are valued, cared about, and respected.

We can't perfect our own hearts, much less those of our children. But surely it is our job as parents to pursue those hearts for the good.

As I've written about these issues over the years, readers have told me how different my views on raising children were from what the experts were saying. A lot of folks thought my views, well, made sense. And so this book came to be.

This is a book that tries to clarify what many parents might instinctively recognize but be afraid to act upon: that ultimately the parenting culture doesn't know more about any one child than his or her own loving parents do. I hope it is a book that will give parents the confidence to raise their children as they see fit, to take from the parenting culture what's helpful, and leave behind, without guilt, what's not—and most of all discern the difference.

It's true that in this book I directly take on the parenting culture in many areas in which I disagree with them. From raising a child's self-esteem, to giving kids choices, to spanking, I critique what the parenting culture teaches the modern mom and dad.

Still, the only important question is, what do *you*, as the parent, think about what the parenting culture teaches the modern mom and dad?

Interestingly, the parenting culture will often use the "right" rhetoric. For instance, some of their leading lights might encourage the idea of parents setting limits. In fact, the notion that parents should be "authoritative" is actually a popular one within certain circles of the parenting culture. Unfortunately, such notions don't seem to mean much to these folks. Because what the experts pay lip service to, on the one hand, and how they actually encourage us to raise our children, on the other, sadly, are often two very different things.

That's why it's so important to get to the nub of what the experts teach about bringing up baby.

As a friend said to me after she read an early draft of this book, "This is really a guide to how to think about what the experts think about raising children." Or maybe "how and why not to be intimidated by the experts."

At least, that was my goal for *It Takes a Parent* when I started to write the book. Now it has taken on an even greater importance. When I began the project I was, I thought, happily married, and I had no reason to believe that situation would ever change.

But I was wrong. To my complete shock, and the shock of everyone who knew and loved my husband—he left our family. Eventually, out of integrity, I was forced to legally dissolve the union of almost seventeen years that my husband had so definitively ended. These events were a tragedy for my children, for me, *and* for my husband. The book, and my life, were both put on hold for months as the children and I grieved.

No one is more opposed to divorce than I am, as I've written many times, and my own experience doesn't change the truth about the devastating impact of divorce, especially on kids. It only makes what I've known to be true about divorce more real, more tangible, more personal.

Maybe that's why, when it became clear that I would be facing life as a single parent (I have sole legal and physical custody of our children), I returned to this manuscript with new eyes on behalf of my kids. As I started to put the pieces of my life back together, I read what I had written and saw it in a new light. The principles I'd cared about for years took on a greater urgency as I faced my new job of raising my children as a single mother. It was more clear to me than ever that how we raise our children, and how we view our role in our children's lives, really matters.

Parents may disagree with many things I say in this book, but I hope they take one thing from it: the confidence to make whatever decisions are right for their own children, because in the end it's their job and only their job to do so. If they see their role in their children's lives as one of persevering to reach their children's hearts, they will have given their children a wonderful gift.

We parents have to decide. Will we accept our calling? Will we dare to parent?

This is not a how-to book, except maybe in the sense of how to think about the experts' advice on child rearing. It's a "What's the right attitude?" book. In a way, it's more about parents than about kids. It's not arranged in chronological order, say, by a child's age; rather, it's arranged in a way that naturally, I hope, unfolds some of the motivation and principles behind reaching a child's heart. Full disclosure: there is nothing in here about toilet training.

Much of what I talk about concerns little ones, because that is, of course, when it's easiest and so most important to establish habits of the heart. But the habit of persevering in our children's lives is one that we'll have long after they're young. It's never too late or too early to apply the principles of this book—if you think they make sense.

Nor is this just a book for married parents or traditional families. This is for anyone who has the responsibility of parenting a child. The practice may get more complicated, a lot more complicated, in different circumstances, but the principles don't change whether we're married or single, older or younger, an adoptive or birth parent, a parent of one or many. Whatever the circumstances in your life, however you run your home, however different it looks from my home, you are the parent. You have been given a great and precious mission—the mission of pursuing your child's heart, of daring to parent, even when the culture tells you not to.

1   Kids Gone Wild

A 2003 *Time* magazine article asked the question "Does Kindergarten Need Cops?" Apparently, the answer is yes. *Time* reported that a first-grader in Fort Worth, Texas, was asked to put a toy away. Instead, she began to scream. "Told to calm down, she knocked over her desk and crawled under the teacher's desk, kicking it and dumping out the contents of the drawers. Then things really began to deteriorate. Still shrieking, the child stood up and began hurling books at her terrified classmates, who had to be ushered from the room to safety."

"Just a bad day at school?" *Time* asked rhetorically. "More like a bad season. The desk-dumping incident followed scores of other outrageous acts by some of the youngest Fort Worth students at schools across the district."

A little one shouting "Shut up, bitch" at a teacher, the biting of another teacher by a kindergartner—so hard it left marks—and a six-year-old who became completely hysterical, took off his clothes, and threw them at the school psychologist are among the highlights.

These are not deeply troubled kids from dysfunctional homes, either. These are normal, healthy kids, many from middle-class, two-parent families, who have not been found to be emotionally disturbed.

Michael Parker is the program director for psychological services at the Fort Worth Independent School District, which serves eighty thousand students. He told *Time* that he's clearly seeing an increase in aggressive behavior from very young children. "We're talking about serious talking back to teachers, profanity, even biting, kicking, and hitting adults, and we're seeing it in five-year-olds."

Houston, we have a problem.

The word "Columbine," the name of the Littleton, Colorado, high school where two boys from upper-middle-class families went on a shooting spree that resulted in thirteen fatalities and the boys' suicides, sends shivers down our collective spines. What happened to those kids? Well, all we really know is that something went terribly wrong a long time before they hit high school.

In 2004, the Partnership for Children, a local child-advocacy group in Fort Worth, released the results of a survey of local elementary schools, child-care centers, and pediatricians. The findings, according to *Time*: almost all of the thirty-nine schools responding reported that kindergartners today have more emotional and behavioral problems than were seen just five years ago. More than half of the day-care centers said incidents of rage and anger had increased over the previous three years.

And it isn't just something in the Texas water.

Dr. Ronald Stephens is the director of the National School Safety Center, based in Westlake, California. Although there is no official reporting mechanism for acts of violence committed by very young children, he told me that the anecdotal evidence is mounting—and showing that behavior problems are rising at a staggering rate. Stephens points to the dramatic increase in the number of alternative schools created for disruptive elementary students in just the past ten years. A decade ago, he says, such schools for the very early elementary grades were virtually unknown; today, at least one thousand of the fifteen thousand school districts in America have them. They are "commonplace and growing," he told me.

Stephens's organization conducts seminars and training for teachers across the country, and anecdotal evidence of kids out of control is common in their workshops. One petite teacher was attacked so viciously by a large six-and-a-half-year-old that she left her job for six months. Another woman, a first-grade teacher for twenty-five years, reported that she literally could not handle some of her current charges because their behavior was so extreme.

A study conducted by the National Association of School Resource Officers (primarily school law enforcement and safety personnel) and released in August 2003 found that more than two-thirds of school police officers believed that younger children were acting more and more aggressively. More than 70 percent of the officers reported an increase in aggressive behavior among elementary schoolchildren in the past five years.

In June 2000, the journal *Pediatrics* released a study of pediatricians with twenty-one thousand patients collectively. The Associated Press summarized things this way: "The number of U.S. youngsters with emotional and behavioral problems has soared in the past two decades."

These increases cannot be dismissed as being due to changes in medical training and diagnosis, said Dr. Kelly Kelleher of the University of Pittsburgh and Children's Hospital, the study's lead author. In fact, according to the AP report, the highest problem-identification rates were by doctors who trained three decades ago and more. Instead, the findings suggest that most of the change was due to "an increase in problems and the kinds of patients they're seeing," Kelleher said. The largest changes were in attention deficit/hyperactivity disorder (ADHD), which increased from 1.4 percent to 9.2 percent, and emotional problems such as anxiety and depression, which increased from negligible to 3.6 percent.

In 2003 alone, more than two million prescriptions were written for antidepressants for children, according to the *Washington Post*.

Of course, the "older generation" has been complaining about "kids gone wild" since the beginning of time. From Socrates to the Puritans—to my own parents, who opposed my girlhood devotion to singer Rod Stewart—we've had laments about how the out-of-control younger generation is always, it seems, worse than ever. But these complaints have traditionally been about the generation coming of age—teenagers and very young adults, not about five- and six-year-olds.

And what about older children and teens? Sadly, we're no longer shocked to hear of such things as an eight-year-old child in the heart of the Midwest—Indianapolis, Indiana—pointing a gun at a classmate because the other child teased him about his ears. Twelve-year-olds in affluent Virginia suburbs outside Washington, D.C., were regularly holding sex parties where oral sex was de rigueur, according to the *Washington Post*. But was anyone *really* surprised?

Teen suicide rates are now the third leading cause of death among fifteen- to twenty-four-year-olds and the fifth leading cause of death among ten- to fourteen-year-olds, according to the American Foundation for Suicide Prevention. In the fifteen to twenty-four age range, suicide rates have tripled for males since 1950, and doubled for females.

There have been widespread rumors about declines in youth violence. But according to a 2001 report from the Surgeon General of the United States, these rumors are not accurate. The report states, "This report has looked beyond arrest and other criminal justice records to several national surveys in which high-school-age youths report in confidence on their violent behavior. These self-reports reveal that the propensity for and actual involvement of youths in serious violence have not declined with arrest rates. Rather, they have remained at the peak rates of 1993."

The report goes on to note that arrest rates for teens committing violent crimes has begun to climb again.

The Far Side of the Spectrum?

Of course, most of what I'm describing is really the extreme, right? Well, yes. After all, thankfully, most six-year-old kids don't beat up their teachers. So these studies and anecdotes describe an increase in problems on the far side of the ledger. But before we collectively breathe easier, we have to admit the scary part: the entire child behavior spectrum has shifted in the wrong direction.

This comment came from a grandmother in Florida who wrote to me in response to a column I'd written on out-of-control kids:

> Today I am very much involved in taking care of the children in the church nursery, and there is a little three-year-old girl who will scream and throw tantrums and throw everything in sight if she is not catered to constantly. The parents of this little girl do cater to her every whim, and they want everyone else to do the same. This little three-year-old is definitely in charge . . .

Such behavior is so common that it's become "the new normal." Every one of us could tell a story like that grandmother's.

I recently took one of my daughters to her gymnastics class. While waiting for the class to start, several children were chasing one another around a small enclosure, and it seemed certain someone was going to get hurt. One mom told her three-year-old, Eric, to walk, not run. Eric continued to race around and around. His mother told him no fewer than five times to stop running. Finally, he slammed into my little Madeleine (who was none the worse for wear, really). Eric's mom said, "Eric, you've had enough. I want you to sit down now!" Eric's response? He looked directly at his mom, got up, and started racing around again. And her response? She and another mom looked at each other, shrugged, and giggled.

Whatever the extenuating circumstances might have been—the mother didn't want a scene or Eric was wound up—one thing is clear: Eric is used to disobeying his mother with impunity. And she is used to it, too.

The New Normal

In a 2004 article on WebMD.com, health reporter Dulce Zamora wrote: "When Junior and his mother walk into the doctor's waiting room, there are two seats available: a big chair for grown-ups and a stool for kids. Junior takes the adult seat and starts to throw a tantrum after Mom asks him to move. With resignation, she squats on the little seat."

Who sits where isn't the issue. The issue is how much power kids wield over their parents. Such scenes are becoming epidemic. If we were doing a reality television show we might call it *Kids Gone Wild!* What's really amazing is not that children attempt such power grabs. Of course they do. It's human nature to want power, and the nature of the hearts children are born with has not changed since Adam and Eve. How they're being raised *has* changed. The parents are too often afraid to address the behavior, and even more so the hearts, of their children.

That's why this book is more about parents than kids.

We could say, Okay, so children today are more badly behaved, more snarly, and more rude. So what? We'll deal with it, we'll ignore it, and we'll get through that phase. After all, most of these kids are not going to grow up to be aberrant, charging into high schools with guns. Living with these kids may be at best unpleasant, at worst miserable—no matter how much we love them—but most will grow up to be some sort of responsible adults. Right?

Well, who knows? But the issue isn't ultimately the behavior, anyway. The behavior reflects what is going on in the child's heart. And it is this heart we must try to reach—and rescue.

On May 22, 2003, the *Wall Street Journal* ran this story on its front page: "Need Help with a Cranky Kid? Frazzled Parents Call a Coach."

> When Amy Griswold's daughter, Ellen, turned three, she began throwing temper tantrums and answering her mother with smart-alecky rejoinders like: "Don't you talk to me that way!"

What else could the Dallas mom do? She called a coach, of course. Writer Barbara Carton went on to explain:

> After months of working with a coach in person, by phone and online, Ms. Griswold is a satisfied customer. To curb Ellen's frequent tantrums when leaving the house, the coach suggested offering dress-up items, such as a tiara, which the preschooler would get to wear after they successfully departed the house. "It eliminated the meltdowns," says Ms. Griswold, who spent about $150 on the coach. "It was worth every penny."

And Mrs. Griswold paid a lot of pennies. That advice cost about $100 an hour.

Think about what this little girl has learned: if she's typically nasty enough, she'll get a prize when she doesn't make others and herself miserable. Here's what her mom has learned: to pay off her daughter to buy peace. But what about when the girl demands a car in exchange for not throwing a tantrum? What happens when she comes across someone, someday, who won't buy her off?

Parent coaches are a growing business. According to the *WSJ* article, the Parent-Coaching Institute of Bellevue, Washington, for instance, opened its doors in 2000; as of summer 2003, it had graduated six coaches and was training twenty-two more.

What About the Heart?

Sure, these kids might grow up to be okay. They might become responsible adults. But what will their hearts, their characters, look like? The little girl in Dallas might grow up to be a normal adult who has a good job, marries, and has children of her own. But what's going on in that "it's all about me" heart of hers? If her parents continue to pay her off to keep her happy, if she grows up learning that her whims will generally be catered to, what will be going on in her heart when she's a "responsible" adult, *if* she's a responsible adult? What kind of marriage will she have? What values will she pass on to her own kids? Will she be able to give, or only to take? I wonder if she will be able to truly find joy.

These aren't questions that evolve simply because a little girl is given a tiara for not throwing a fit. Every parent blows it sometimes—or, in my case, a lot of times. But Ellen is being raised to think the world is all about her. The tiaras are just a symptom of a much larger problem— one with potentially devastating consequences.

Dr. Robert Shaw is a practicing child psychiatrist in Berkeley, California. In his bold 2003 book *The Epidemic: The Rot of American Culture, Absentee and Permissive Parenting, and the Resultant Plague of Joyless, Selfish Children,* he writes this:

Far too many children today are sullen, unfriendly, distant, preoccupied and even unpleasant. They whine, nag, throw tantrums, and demand constant attention from their parents. . . . Many kids, even very young ones, treat their parents with contempt, rolling their eyes and speaking rudely. . . . The behavior of these discontented, joyless children is so common these days that many people no longer consider it abnormal. We rationalize it, normalize it, and call it a "phase" or a "stage" at each point along the way.

Joyless children. The new normal. Something is wrong with this picture.

More Paid-Off Kids—More Depression?

In his powerful book *The Progress Paradox*, science writer Gregg Easterbrook looks at the fact that in the West, and particularly in the United States, we have ease of life, physical health, leisure time, political freedom, and life spans unimaginable in previous generations. And yet, not only have rates of happiness not gone up in fifty years, rates of depression have skyrocketed, rising ten times since 1950. Surely, some of this is due to better reporting and the decreasing stigma attached to depression. But, like most experts, Easterbrook believes that there has been, in fact, a significant increase in depression in the past fifty years.

People who suffer from depression need help, not condemnation. But is the rise in depression symptomatic of larger problems that plague our culture? Yes, says Dr. Martin Seligman, a psychologist at the University of Pennsylvania and past president of the American Psychological Association. Seligman, who himself largely pioneered the academic study of happiness, says there are four main reasons for the rise in depression rates in the United States. The first is that "rampant individualism causes us to think that our setbacks are of vast importance and thus something to become depressed about."

Seligman blames the self-esteem craze, too. The emphasis on self-esteem has made millions of people think there's something wrong with them if they don't feel good about themselves at any given moment, versus a more balanced rational approach: "I don't feel good about myself right now, but I will later." The two other causes of depression, according to Seligman, are the "teaching of victimology and helplessness" and runaway consumerism. (From *The Progress Paradox*.)

Memo to parents: Wake up!

Meanwhile, maybe, just maybe, even some parenting experts may be starting to think we have a problem. In the article "Are You a Parent or a Pushover?" in the January 2004 issue of *Parents* magazine, Kellye Carter Crocker reported on a *Parents* survey in which most mothers expressed "deep concern over today's discipline methods." Eighty-eight percent of these mothers said parents "let children get away with too much," although only 40 percent thought that problem applied to their own kids. The math seems a little implausible, but the point is an important one.

Magazine surveys may be notoriously inaccurate, but this one reveals some level of angst over how kids are being raised. As Crocker writes, parents may be "sensing what mounting evidence is starting to reveal: Some of the discipline strategies that have been in vogue in recent years just aren't working. Elaborate systems that give kids multiple chances, prolonged discussions about the 'feelings' behind bad behavior, negotiations about consequences and so on are often ineffective."

Yet, such strategies are still the mainstay of the parenting culture.

That's why this book is more about parents than children. Out-of-control kids very often come from parents who are not in control. They may be wonderful, giving, generous people who are devoted to their children. But too many of them are like the mom and her parenting coach, who think it's a great idea to pay off a preschooler just for not throwing a huge fit.

The following is a recent advice column from Parents.com, the website of *Parents* magazine. Forget the answers; it's the questions from these typically loving, educated, middle-class moms and dads that tell us how kids are being raised today.

Q: When I ask my four-and-a-half-year-old to do something like set the table or clean up his toys, he insists he's busy or just says "no"! What should I do?

Q: Our three-year-old loves to boss us around. If I say, "Let's wear white socks," she says, "Blue!" If I say, "Let's brush our teeth," she says, "No! Pajamas first!" We want her to feel like she has a say, but this is getting ridiculous!

Q: Bedtime has become an exhausting ordeal. My son always needs one more thing—another story, a glass of water, a different blanket. How can I get him to stay in bed?

Q: I can never have an uninterrupted phone conversation! Every time the phone rings, my daughter makes a fuss or clings to me like glue.

Q: My three-year-old has started to cry whenever she can't get her way. Should I just ignore her?

You get the picture—and it's not a pretty one. These are caring parents, but they are not portraits of parental courage, which is exactly what their kids need them to be if the children are going to have their hearts shaped for the good.

As perfectly spoiled Veruca so aptly puts it in *Willy Wonka & the Chocolate Factory* (which I've watched at least eighty-seven times with my kids, so I know the dialogue by heart), "But I want it *now*, Daddy!"

And every time, Daddy complies with "Veruca dear's" commands because he doesn't want to cause her any distress.

This is a father who is poisoning his child's heart.

The "heart" issue is fundamental to everything I discuss in this book.

I once heard a Christian speaker give a fine talk on effective discipline. She had some good ideas, and she boasted that her children were so well-behaved that they were the delight of the church nursery. Her children, their proper behavior, and her effective discipline were a source of great pride to her. But I do not remember her talking about their hearts.

What was her purpose in addressing their behavior? What was her purpose in effective discipline? No doubt, expecting good behavior is a good and necessary thing in training our children. But, if our focus is primarily manipulating our children's behavior effectively, it's possible we'll only succeed in teaching them that behaving a certain way is nothing more than *the ticket* to whatever it is they wanted in the first place, even if it's just the goodwill of Mom and Dad. If we end up just helping them to learn to manipulate their world to reach their own selfish ends—instead of helping to train their hearts to delight in goodness because it is delightful—well then, it's even possible that we've helped shaped those hearts for the worse.

Tedd Tripp discusses this at length in *Shepherding a Child's Heart*. He talks about parents who eagerly try each new discipline method as it rolls out from the parenting culture's pipeline. He considers how such methods might achieve the right outward behavior, for a time, but not fundamentally change the selfish tendencies of the child's heart.

One method, for instance, is to put a piece of paper in a jar each time a child does something she's asked to do and take one out each time she disobeys. After a specified period, if there are a certain number of slips in the jar, the child gets a prize. As Tripp points out, this is an easy trick to figure out. She learns to watch the scales of right and wrong behavior, and makes very sure that "right" is always tipped just a bit more in her direction. The child has learned how to manipulate her world.

If she's at all bright, she'll quickly figure out that if she saves up enough "good" chits, why, she can indulge in some bad behavior and still come out "ahead." She hasn't learned to disdain disobedience at all; she's just learned how the game works. She hasn't come to see that obeying her parents is a blessing to her and to them—she hasn't learned to love being a blessing.

In another example from Tripp's book, two siblings fight over a toy one has taken from the other. Yes, there's a matter of justice that needs to be addressed, but the wronged child is still putting his "right" to the toy above his relationship with his sibling. What will these children learn if their parents address only the behavior, and not the heart issue behind it?

Throughout *It Takes a Parent,* I'll look at ways that, I hope, are effective in reaching the hearts of our children. In chapter 12, "To Spank or Not to Spank," I'll consider discipline methods and how some may be more effective than others at reaching the heart of a child. But before I even get to those things, I'll need to convince you that we need to be on a rescue mission for our children's hearts.

A Rescue Mission

Our children are born into a world that is bent on capturing their hearts and minds, and most certainly not for their good. Yes, I think the world is full of good things, and I don't think we have to shut the culture out as much as we have to help our kids think rightly about it. But there is no question that the world seeks to win our children over to its way of thinking and behaving, and the world does not love our children.

We do.

More important, we need to see that children must be rescued from themselves. This truth is not something with which the parenting culture is comfortable.

A principal of a parochial school in an affluent suburb of Chicago wrote to tell me what he sees on a daily basis, and it doesn't look like parents on a rescue mission for the hearts of their children:

- When children receive detention for being tardy, parents often ask to serve in their place, even if it was solely the child's dawdling that made him late.
- Parents of a four-year-old conference-called the child at school about his behavior.
- A four-year-old was allowed to choose the school he would attend.
- Another four-year-old stole an earring from a department store. The mother and child returned the earring, and then the mother took the child to a toy store to buy a treat because the child had done the right thing in returning the stolen earring.
- A mother decided not to send her child to a school that served only white milk, because her child would drink only chocolate milk.

Here again is why this book is more about parents than kids.

Full disclosure: as I write this book, I find that I'm one of those parents being called to account on my rescue mission. When I lived in Virginia, my ten-year-old niece visited me with her dad, my brother. Later, she told him how amazed she was to watch Aunt Betsy completely caving in to little Madeleine, giving her something she demanded, just to get Madeleine to stop whining. Apparently, this incident demolished my niece's view of me as running a tight ship. And this has possibly happened, um, more than once, because I didn't even remember the particular incident.

I'm not worried that someday Madeleine is going to be a juvenile delinquent because I gave in to her on that occasion (and apparently quite a few others). But it's also true for all of us that being more aware of how we interact with our kids, determining what's the norm in our home and what's the exception, is the first step in helping our kids.

I hardly think all behavior problems are the result of out-of-control or ineffective parents. Sometimes there are underlying medical or emotional problems, which I'll discuss later. Some of these are becoming more common, and some are becoming better identified. A small percentage of children, although healthy, are so extraordinarily strong willed that, despite the parents' best efforts, the child remains consistently angry and defiant. Parents of these kids sometimes just want to give up. I hope this book will encourage them to try to stay engaged.

Nor am I suggesting that the parenting culture thinks such behaviors as those I've described in this chapter are a good thing. Certainly many bright lights of the parenting culture would bemoan the very same behaviors and attitudes that I've chronicled. They might even speak to the need for parents to intervene. But as I've said before, what the parenting culture generally pays lip service to on the one hand, and how it actually encourages us to raise our children on the other, are, sadly, often two very different things.

So, What's Going On?

Is it perhaps that our culture is more stressed than in previous times? Sure, these things can have an impact. But living during the Depression or World War II would have been far more stressful than living in the "rush-rush" 2000s. In those periods in our history, many Americans experienced severe deprivation and uncertainty; but there is not the evidence of widespread child behavior problems like those we see today.

It's also true that American culture has coarsened terribly, and I'm the first to bemoan it. Particularly for middle-schoolers and high-schoolers, the popular culture can be downright ugly, with depictions of violence and sex everywhere. Even children's cartoons and television shows are filled with kids disdaining one another and their parents. *Rugrats* and *The Fairly Odd Parents* are just a couple of examples that come to mind.

Finding a G-rated move with no sexual innuendo or cynicism is increasingly difficult. In PG, it's impossible. Such things were rife, for instance, in the wildly popular (and yes, quite clever and entertaining) movie *Shrek,* and graphic in the "kids'" movie *Scooby-Doo.*

But, as parents, our job is to control what our kids see, not to blame what they see for a lack of our own hands-on attention. As our children grow older and by choice or necessity we no longer control what they watch or hear, our job is to help them think rightly about the culture, what they absorb, and what they should want to absorb.

The authors of the *Pediatrics* study I referred to earlier partially blamed increases in divorce, single-parent households, and dependence on public assistance for behavior problems. But even these problems go back to the parents and how one or both of them are—or are not—interacting with their children. It's also clear, by the way, that there are many wonderful parents (single *and* sometimes married) who are doing everything they can to make up for the neglect of the other parent.

That has to have a huge impact for the good.

It Takes a Parent—and a Village—
to Raise a Child

In one sense, I believe it does take a village to raise a child. For instance, my divorce is not just my business. It's a pebble in a stream and has a huge effect on others in the community, including on how children down my own street may come to view the permanence, or impermanence, of marriage. When both parents in the home around the corner work so many hours that their unhappy child goes to another family's home for companionship, his problems become that family's problems, too. We are not islands, and the way we adults lead our lives affects the children all around us. We have a responsibility to the little ones in our lives, not just the ones in our own family, to do the right thing. That's why there really isn't such a thing as "privacy" after all.

I would love to magically fix all the negative aspects of our culture— but I can't. I would love to eradicate pornography from the web, get rid of gratuitous violence in the media and popular music, and restore images of virtue and strong family lives in film and television.

But I can't do all those things. I can't change the externals in the neighborhood or in the popular culture, at least not to my satisfaction. I couldn't even wave a magic wand to put my family back together, although I would have loved to. The thing I can do as a parent is to try to think and act rightly when it comes to parenting my own kids—to persevere in what I'm called to do—and trust that that will have an impact.

That's why this book is more about parents than kids.

There's good news, too. I often hear via e-mail and letters from great kids, teenagers in particular, who remind me that many terrific kids out there are as appalled at some of the behavior of their peers as I am. I'm not saying there is such a thing as the "perfect teenager" and what, exactly, would that be anyway? But I am talking about kids who openly love and honor their parents, who even think their parents are pretty cool. Kids who are intent on doing the right things in their lives and not giving in to the culture around them. Kids who give of themselves to others, who make a difference, who are examples to their friends. I am proud to say I know many such young people.

These young people have something in common: parents (or sometimes another loving adult in their lives) who are challenging the culture when it comes to raising their children. These parents are doing an awesome job. Such parents and other caring adults don't get the media play troubled parents or parents of troubled kids do, but they are noble. Their stories, whether I know them personally or learn of them through readers of my column, are an incredible encouragement to me and should be an incredible encouragement to all of us. They are making a difference in their children's lives and in their community's life.

I hope this book will encourage them, too.

These parents are persevering—and that's what the next chapter is about. Perseverance in reaching and shaping and rescuing the hearts of our children. Our duty is to persevere as parents, no matter what discouraging stories we hear, no matter what is going on around us, to persevere with a great hope that if we "train up a child in the way he should go . . . when he is old he will not depart from it" (Proverbs 22:6).

Parenting Check

You probably breathed a sigh of relief knowing that your child would never kick a teacher. But what about the child at gymnastics class ignoring his mother's instructions? Did you see yourself there? What about the questions parents wrote to the parenting magazine? Are questions like those too often your questions, too?

Some of this happens in all of our homes—mine, too. The questions are: Are we aware of the power struggles our children attempt and are we actively engaged in responding appropriately? Or are their struggles, and our capitulation to them, so common that it's become the new normal?

What about the heart issue? Is this the first time you've thought that it might be possible to get the right behavior but not be rightly training or encouraging the heart of your child?

2 Perseverance: Mission Possible

W*ebster's Dictionary* defines perseverance as "persistence in a state, enterprise, or undertaking in spite of counterinfluences, opposition, or discouragement." Whatever perseverance looks like in your home, it's great parenting.

Judith Rich Harris doesn't believe there's a point in parental perseverance. She does not think that parents have an impact on their children over the long term. Harris authored the controversial and provocative 1998 book *The Nurture Assumption: Why Children Turn Out the Way They Do*. She writes: "This book has two purposes: first, to dissuade you of the notion that a child's personality—what used to be called 'character'—is shaped or modified by the child's parents; and second, to give you an alternative view of how the child's personality is shaped." She argues that only peers, not parents, shape a child.

By far the most interesting thing about Harris's book is that it caused a sensation when it stormed onto the national scene, probably because it let many parents off the hook. These were parents who felt powerless anyway, and they wanted to rationalize their inaction. "Imparentency" one might call such a view.

Of course, parents most likely can't turn an academic child into a sports nut, or a shy little one into an extrovert, or a budding artist into a mechanic. Who would want to? The more we learn about genetics, the more we learn that genes can interact to influence whether a child is a risk taker or overly cautious or even predisposed to happiness or sullenness.

Anyone who has had more than one child sees personality differences from the start. In fact, many of us could sense personality differences in the womb. Even Harris doesn't offer clear answers to the nature-versus-nurture debate. She maintains that while well-mannered, competent people might produce well-mannered, competent children, for instance, this could be because the parents passed on their good genes, not their good social skills. But she says it's impossible to tease out the ultimate answer with the information we have now. Essentially, she leaves it at "Who knows?"

One interesting consequence of Harris's theory that children are shaped primarily by peer pressure is that all those adults who blame their parents for their moral shortcomings on the analyst's couch can now complain about their "controlling peer groups" instead.

Still, Harris's book was something of a welcome respite from the folks who terrorize parents into believing that if they don't bond with their child in the first hours after birth, carry them around in a sling, play Beethoven and give them other extraordinary stimulation in the first three years of life, all with the goal of raising the child's all-important self-esteem, the child—and, by extension, the parents—will be failures.

Harris says parents influence their young children in the home, in the preschool years, but she focuses on the child over the long term. The problem is that there, she says, parents are impotent.

There it is again—"imparentancy."

Harris's book was both praised and denounced by experts, but it contains a fatal flaw. Harris essentially equates personality with character, when in fact they are two very different things.

Personality Does Not Character Make

The concept that personality is not the same thing as character seems alien to our culture today. Yet while we each have different inborn traits, desires, ways of expressing ourselves, patterns of behavior, even ways of thinking, that is *not* the sum total of who we are. Our natural impulses or leanings need not dictate our behavior as if we were animals. In fact, what makes us human and different from every other animal is precisely the ability to control, or at least genuinely attempt to control, when and whether and how and how much to express may of those inborn traits. And, when we fail, we have the ability to try to do better the next time.

Time magazine got it right in a 1998 article, "The Personality of Genes." The article focused on biologist Dean Hamer, a leading researcher in behavioral genetics, the study of how genes influence behavior. (Hamer and colleague Peter Copeland coauthored *Living with Our Genes* in 1998.)

As the scientists explain it, when it comes to genes that give tomatoes their flavor, for instance, even a simple trait like acidity isn't controlled by a single gene but by *dozens* of genes that work together and impact one another in the process. In the same way, many genes are involved in the setup of even a single temperamental trait. And "ultimately, it is the environment that determines how these genes will express themselves. . . . What people are born with, Hamer says, are temperamental traits. What they can acquire through experience is the ability to control these traits by exercising that intangible part of personality called character."

So character—something very different than personality—counts after all.

Parents Matter

And it seems that parents, whether they like it or not, can have a lot to do with shaping character.

A study from Ohio State University, published in the August 1999 issue of the journal *Criminology,* found that throughout adolescence, parents continue to have a significant impact on whether their kids engage in delinquent behavior. The study looked at seventeen hundred students over five years and found that where the influence of school and peers ebbs and flows, with peer-group pressure peaking at around age 13½, parental influence stays constant. Dr. Sung Joon Jang, lead author of the study and assistant professor of sociology at Ohio State, said, "People tend to perceive parents as likely losers in competition with their children's friends over influencing adolescent behavior. . . . But this study shows that parents still have an impact throughout adolescence on whether their children become involved in delinquent behavior."

Child Trends, an independent, nonpartisan research center in Washington, D.C., found that when parents were regularly involved in religious activities, their adolescents were more likely to exhibit fewer behavior problems and greater social responsibility. A study that appeared in the April/June 2000 issue of the *Journal of Applied Developmental Psychology* found that a child is most likely to accept his parents' religious beliefs when his relationship with his folks is a warm one, and when he believes that the religious commitment is very important to his parents.

Even Judith Harris admits that religion is an area where parents can have an impact on their kids. Talk about character building.

Okay, parents influence their kids when it comes to delinquency and religion. What about sex? There, too, Mom and Dad matter. Particularly Mom, and particularly when it comes to girls. In September 2002, the *Journal of Adolescent Health* reported on a study of three thousand mother-teen pairs. The study found that teenage girls who have a close relationship with their mothers wait longer to have sex for the first time. The girls were also less likely to have sex if their mothers strongly disapproved of it, according to University of Minnesota researcher Clea McNeely, who led the study, and her colleagues. (In this review, the moms did not appear to have an impact on their sons' sex lives, and fathers were not included in the analysis.)

Finally, the federal government's latest National Household Survey on Drug Use and Health (2003) reported that when it comes to drugs, substance abuse was definitely lower among kids who believed their parents would strongly disapprove of it.

So, parents influence—often strongly—even their teens when it comes to drugs, sex, delinquent behavior, and religious attitudes. Is it so hard to imagine, then, that parents can strongly influence whether their four-year-old routinely sends macaroni and cheese flying across a restaurant table? Of course they can. Even Harris agrees with that much.

Nature vs. Nurture?
Not the Right Question!

If I see a young child throwing a fit in the toy store because he's not getting the toy he wants, and the parents are standing by impotent and helpless, I look to the parents, not the little guy, to explain what's happening. Sure, it's possible that the child has an emotional or psychological problem but, generally, I would be inclined to say that Mom and Dad have fallen down on the job.

But the blame will not stay with the parents. As the child grows, he will take on more and more responsibility for his actions and moral choices. Even if he is terribly hindered by years of bad or nonexistent training, a sad situation to be sure, he will still be responsible for the adult he becomes. And there are many stories of wonderful people emerging from very bad training.

Alternatively, even great parents, who do all the right things (whatever that means)—including not letting their children get in the habit of throwing fits in toy stores or sending their macaroni and cheese flying across restaurant tables—are not guaranteed great kids. Their children may have had the tremendous benefit of good training, but if they fail as adults, the fact they had good training will only add to their moral culpability.

So we're left with this: We parents can have a tremendous shaping influence on our children. But in the end, we cannot wholly determine the kind of people they become or the kind of hearts they will develop. There may be mitigating or aggravating circumstances in the way they were raised, but one day they will have to take moral responsibility for who they are.

And that's why the nature/nurture question isn't really the right one to ask. We aren't promised a perfect "end product" when it comes to our children, regardless of whether it's nature or nurture that gets them there.

What Is a Persevering Parent?

Parents cannot determine good outcomes for their children. What we *can* determine is whether we will persevere to the best of our ability in training and guiding them toward the right end. All we can really know is that our perseverance is the best hope of seeing them reach a whole-some adulthood.

In many ways, this truth can be encouraging. At times, we all fail as parents. We're tired, so we don't discipline when we should. We yell when we shouldn't. We're impatient, or we get frustrated, or we lose our tempers. I'm not letting us off the hook, but I'm pointing out the obvious: we may have failures along the way, but they need not be fatal. In fact, if we understand our mission to persevere in our children's lives, those failures can encourage us to redouble our efforts toward the larger goal we are pursuing.

When my Olivia was two (which happened to be the same year I was writing this book), she had a great time at her little one-morning-a-week Bible school. On the last day of class in June, each parent received a note from the teacher about his or her child. This is what the teacher wrote about Olivia: "She loves to sing and dance during song time. She is extremely helpful when it's clean-up time. She does not, however, like to be told that she cannot have or do something that she has set her mind on. This should be something to work on before September."

What was I going to say? "Um, look, as soon as I finish writing my book on parenting, I'll work with Olivia on her social skills"? No. I just sort of skulked out, mumbling something about how I appreciated all that the teacher had done for Olivia.

That was a call for me to persevere with my youngest!

Alternatively, there are times when our children fail. We firmly believe we are on the right path—and they disappoint us. We accept our position of authority in their lives and we've used it to talk with them, to appropriately discipline them, to reason with them, to appeal to their hearts—all in the best sense of these terms—and we're not seeing the fruit of our investment.

But if we understand that our purpose is to persevere, especially when we don't see in our kids what we would like to see at the moment, then we can focus on our duty to persevere instead of focusing on their behavior at that moment. By focusing on what we *can* control—our perseverance as parents—we can turn a discouraging moment into an encouraging one.

It Takes a Parent differs from most other books on parenting because it does not promise a better kid. In our results-oriented society, we want promises. We want to believe that if we just save up enough good-parenting chits, we can turn them in for happy, successful, emotionally fit children. If only it were that easy.

At the beginning of the twentieth century, when the "science" of child rearing was being discovered, it was truly thought that we could remake children in the image we created for them. A hundred years and reams of wildly conflicting advice from the experts later, we're still looking for that promise. Consider these recent book titles: *How to Raise Happy, Confident Kids; Resourcefulness Parenting: How to Raise Happy, Successful Kids; A Grateful Father's Story: How to Raise Healthy, Happy Kids; How to Raise Happy, Loving, Emotionally Intelligent Kids*. In fact, if you input anything about "raising great kids" into Amazon.com, you will get almost four hundred responses. Now, it's true that some of that has to do with puppies and sex lives and other things one wouldn't have thought of, but the fact remains there are *a lot* of books on how to raise terrific little ones.

We want guarantees. But the only thing we really know is that we have a duty as parents to persevere. And that in that perseverance lies the best hope for our children. I liken this approach to an elite military rescue team. Each team member must focus on his job. He cannot think, "Gee, the odds on this one seem tough [even when they are], so I won't do my job to the fullest. I mean, that requires a lot of work, and I'm tired of the whole thing. We're not seeing short-term results anyway." Nor does he say to his commanding officer, "I'll do my best if you promise me that in the end our mission will be successful." Instead, the team member's duty is to persevere even in the face of death. He knows that persevering provides the best chance of success and that not doing so will almost certainly lead to failure. Even more, he knows that doing his duty well and wholeheartedly is the only thing for which he can take full responsibility.

That's what this book is about—persevering in doing the right things for our children. Here there are no promises of "Ten Instant Tantrum Tamers," "Stop Tantrums in Sixty Seconds Flat," or "Three Easy Rules for Sibling Peace"—all titles of recent parenting-magazine articles. After reading an article like that, how do you feel if the tantrums don't stop after sixty seconds? That's when parents get discouraged. Instead, they should *trust themselves* to decide the right way to engage their kids, and then persevere, even if it doesn't work in sixty seconds.

Sure, we parents need to deal appropriately with taming our children's passions. But, more important, we have to try to reach their hearts and shape their character for a lifetime.

Training Day

Every day is training day. A top tennis player is trained to respond a certain way. His training is so regular, so consistent, that it becomes a part of him. So when he's on the court for a title match, he doesn't have to think, "I'll run over to the right and swing, now I'll go to the left," and so on. He responds without having to think.

An amazing thing occurs with athletes who train at the top levels of speed sports such as downhill racing. They actually take in information much faster than a typical person. So, for example, a ski racer going down the mountain at eighty miles an hour will tell you that, while his speed is breathtaking, he sees the gates and calculates his turns in slow motion. His training takes over.

Or we could be talking about an excellent pianist who masters a piece by practicing it hundreds of times, learning it so thoroughly that it's as if her fingers guide her. Even if her conscious mind is not fully engaged, her hands will play the music beautifully.

Training can take over when it comes to the heart, too.

Bruce Ismay, president of the White Star Line, was on his company's ill-fated *Titanic* when it sank in 1912. Although the "women and children first" order had gone out, Ismay took an empty seat on a lifeboat. The reports of his behavior are conflicting, but the evidence is that he *didn't* take a seat from a woman or a child—though we know he certainly *did* take precedence over other potential male passengers because of his status. In any case, by taking a seat to save himself, he risked doing more harm, including possibly causing a break in the remaining ranks and chaos, or even swamped lifeboats. This could have cost more lives.

His character may never have been tested until that moment, but when it mattered most, he showed how a lifetime of training had molded his heart. Bruce Ismay made it to New York alive, but for a number of reasons related to the *Titanic* sinking, he spent the rest of his life in disgrace.

Flash forward to September 11, 2001. Todd Beamer was also on an ill-fated vessel, United Airlines Flight 93. He and several other passengers exhibited incredible bravery in storming the cockpit, hoping to somehow land the plane but knowing that they were probably going to their doom. They wanted to save whomever they could on the ground. Their bravery may have kept that plane from a devastating assault on the Capitol or the White House. The hearts of Todd Beamer and the other passengers acting with him were also trained over the course of their lifetimes. They, too, might never have been truly tested before, but when the moment came, their characters took over, characters that had been molded—trained—for the good.

What will happen when our children's characters are tested? When the heart behind the behavior of the moment is revealed?

We may not want to think that every day is training day, but it is. Every day our children's hearts are being trained for or against the good. That's not easy to think about when we've got errands to run, bills to pay, work to do, and kids to get to soccer practice. Nor can we beat ourselves up if we don't have a perfectly persevering day. News flash: No parent I know, especially me, has *ever* had a perfectly persevering day. We're talking the long term, here.

Such big issues are not always fun to think about. Let's face it—we want to enjoy our kids. They're a blast much of the time and a blessing all the time. It's easier and more pleasant to just have fun with them— and we should. Few things make me happier than hanging around with my kids. Whether it's a summer afternoon matinee, eating ice cream at the pool, or getting "school reports" from them at dinner, my children are a delight to my heart. Yes, there are times when they can be really annoying, too, but I'm talking big picture.

Anyway, in the midst of all this, we can't lose sight of their hearts. Understood rightly, it's not a chore but a pleasure. Knowing that every day is training day can make even the miniature golf, the movie, or the hanging around more fun and more meaningful. Such moments can take on a wonderful significance.

The notion of "training day" even gives meaning to those really annoying moments.

I often hear, "I wish I knew how to play the piano. I took lessons as a kid, but my parents never made me practice." There could be a host of practical reasons that one might start a child in piano lessons and then decide it's not worth pursuing. And some kids are so overscheduled, the last thing they need is one more activity. Still, an adult who says, "My parents didn't make me practice," is one small and, I suppose, not terribly consequential example of parents not persevering. (I mean, if your child is going to take piano lessons, she ought to practice.) But there are other consequences to not perservering that are far more serious.

Sadly, I see parents who have given up on their kids. They love them, they want the best for them, and they hope they turn out well. But in small and sometimes large ways, they have stopped persevering. Maybe they've given up getting their little one to limit his tantrums, hoping it's a phase. Maybe they think there's no way they can stop their eight-year-old from speaking rudely to them, so they don't try. Maybe they know their fourteen-year-old lies to them about where she's going, but they stop confronting her because it creates such a scene.

Whether it's just one bad attitude or a particular behavior the parents think they can't influence anymore or whether it's the whole child, these parents stopped persevering when the going got tough. They've given up on their duty to their child.

I've caught myself not persevering countless times in day-to-day matters. I may have great plans for my children to memorize Bible verses, get better about picking up after themselves, or go to the art museum at least once every six weeks. I was committed to teaching my oldest to read at age four. Other times, I've promised myself that my kids wouldn't watch TV for an entire month, that they would do educational crafts instead. I've had much sillier notions, too, but we all have lists like that.

Sometimes I've had to say, "This doesn't work at this point in our lives" (the art museum idea). Sometimes I've had to restart something for the six thousandth time (memorizing Bible verses). Sometimes I just keep plugging away (picking up after themselves). And sometimes I have to admit that an idea is ridiculous (educational crafts instead of TV or teaching my four-year-old to read). And there are times I've failed in ways *much* bigger than not getting my kids to the art museum every six weeks.

One weekend afternoon, I was out for an hour or so doing research for my book while my husband, Ben, was home with the kids. When I returned and pulled onto our street, I saw a stranger standing by the curb, holding Olivia, who was then about two and a half. Turns out, she was waiting for the police to arrive. Why had she called the police? My littlest one had been all by herself on the street in front of our old home for several minutes. It was a quiet cul-de-sac with only four houses, but it fed onto a busier street. A kind woman had seen Olivia and stopped to help.

Moments later, after I'd determined that my baby was okay, the police pulled in. The absurdity of the situation hit me: *Officer, as bad as this looks, it's really okay, because I was out researching my book on parenting.* Yikes. Besides, it wasn't okay. I was furious at Ben. When I started to tell the officer that I'd just pulled into the street and my husband was in the house watching the kids, he replied, "Would you like my nightstick to use on him?" I said no thanks, but wondered silently if he was using his revolver at the moment. I calmed down pretty fast, though, because really this wasn't about Ben. The same thing could have happened if I were home, watching the kids, but just became distracted for a few minutes.

That incident called Ben and me to account and taught us to be a lot more careful with our youngest. We'd been careless in assuming she was safe because she couldn't open the doors leading outside herself. Well, she wasn't safe—as we learned when we realized she'd gotten out by following a neighbor child out the front door. Then, it was a physical issue of whether she could open doors and whether she understood the rules about going outside. Later, issues like driving, drugs, and sex will be far more serious. That incident was a call to persevere.

Some things in our day-to-day lives are more important than others in the long term. I do the best I can to sort out which is which—and no matter what, keep moving forward in spite of failures small and large.

This isn't to say we can't reevaluate the best way to reach our children's hearts and make changes or apply different strategies at different times to reach them. For example, I've persevered in teaching my children from the time they could talk how to address adults. I tell them they must use names and look into the person's eyes. I've told them that it helps adults understand that we care about them and respect them.

In training my kids to be able to strike up a respectful, engaged conversation, I've used many strategies. Sometimes I use role-playing: "Pretend I'm Mrs. Schneider, and you've just walked into my house. What do you say?" At other times, I use humor: "Okay, guys, whatever you do, when we go to the Bells' house, do not speak to them! Look at their kneecaps, and make sure you ignore them!" (That always cracks them up.) Often I use reminders (hoping they'll beat me to it to avoid embarrassment): "Remember to thank Mrs. Fairbanks for your lesson, dear."

Still, when I ask, "Did you say good-bye and thank you, and did you use Mrs. Carlson's name?" I often hear, "Um, no, Mom, I forgot." Sigh. But I'm persevering in my goal. Although I'm using different strategies at different times and with different kids, my purpose is singular: to reach their hearts to help shape them so that they notice, appreciate, and respect others. Knowing I can bank only on that perseverance and not on my children's response encourages me to keep at it.

There are more and less direct ways of getting to the heart, and they might vary with each child, but getting there is the mission. We have to ask ourselves, Is our purpose to reach the heart of our child?

Does Perseverance Matter?

Here's a letter I received from a high-school guidance counselor in response to a column I'd written on the growing trend of adult children moving back in with Mom and Dad:

> I have been a high-school guidance counselor for twenty-six years. The changes I've observed in teenagers and parents and their relationship has been truly amazing. It's exactly as you describe.

No matter how hard I try to convince parents that they need to be the one in charge and follow through on rules and expectations, I must admit I've had little success, especially these last ten years. Parents have abdicated their parental responsibilities and instead become their child's friend and financial backer. It is rare to have a parent with high expectations, a set of structured rules, and a strong moral foundation to guide their child.

My observations tell me that this coming generation is the most spoiled and least thankful of any generation thus far. They expect everyone to give them everything. We are destroying our future generations by taking away from them the value of having to earn what they value.

This counselor is describing parents who did not persevere. Parents who loved their children, who were devoted to their children, but who did not believe that they were on a rescue mission for their children's hearts. Parents who did not understand that they were called to persevere in that mission even when—especially when—they couldn't be guaranteed the mission's outcome. Even when—especially when—they were discouraged. The parents didn't know, or didn't believe, or didn't care enough that persevering in that rescue mission was the best hope of saving that child.

Even worse, these parents trained their children in the wrong things. If we regularly train our children to let their passions rule them— whether it's something as awful as attacking a teacher or as ordinary as throwing macaroni and cheese across the table or rolling eyes in disgust at Mom or Dad—it's a good bet that at moments of testing, in large ways or small, these children will not be portraits of courage.

I also wonder, will they be joyful givers or just takers?

If we train our children to do the right things, if we train them to want and delight in the right things, it's much more likely that in a moment of testing, their hearts—trained and fit for the purpose at hand—will respond as we might hope. And whether we give them enough practice largely depends on whether we persevere as parents in our duty to our kids.

Parenting Check

We parents often tend to gauge our parenting by our child's behavior, not our own perseverance as parents. Do you see how that can cause a lot of unnecessary discouragement to us and to our children?

What do you think of the notion that each day we are, in some way, training our children, for good or ill? Is there some area of your child's behavior or character where you've just given up because you haven't seen the results you've wanted? How can you reorient your thinking to reengage your child in that area?

3

I'm on Your Side (What's a Parent for, Anyway?)

I'm on your side." Imagine how much easier our job as parents would be if our kids really believed that we're on their side, we're their advocates, we back them.

Most parents have figured out that it's great to be on their child's side, but the way many parents get there is backward. In our culture, "I'm on your side" has come to mean "I'll give to you, or do for you, or give in to you—whatever you want. Just please accept me. Please acknowledge me. Please like me. Please be nice to me. Please *let* me be on your side."

When I say, "I'm on your side," I'm talking about just the opposite of such an approach. I'm talking about a parent who is willing to wrestle with his child for the heart of that child, as if that child's very life and soul are at stake. Because they are.

One of my daughters was giving me a hard time. There was a hint of snideness, a touch of irritation, and a pinch of "I know better than you," all smothered in "Mom, nothing you do is good enough." I turned to her, lifted her chin, and looked her directly in the eye. In an adamant voice, I said, "Under no circumstances may you act like that to me. Other families may allow their little girls to behave in a rude way or use a snide voice to their parents, but not here. I love you too much to let you get in the habit of being surly. And that's what it is, a habit. Is that clear?"

Clear or not, it was a response she had heard from me before, and she wasn't happy about it. She nodded her head as tears welled up and announced she was going to bed. A minute later, I went after her.

I sat on her bed and held her stiffened body. I didn't let her pull away. I said, "Darling, I would lay down my life for you. I wouldn't even have to think about it. So if I have to wrestle with you from time to time to keep you from developing habits of the heart that will be destructive to you, I will do it in a minute. That's a no-brainer for me, because I love you too much to do anything else. I'm on your side."

Her body softened slightly. And a few minutes later, we were back downstairs, lying entwined on the sofa and consoling each other as we watched the Chicago Cubs lose a big game.

I hardly go into this level or explanation every time something like this happens. And one thing I *didn't* do was to ask her why she was behaving the way she was. Kids almost never know why they do the upsetting things that they do. Let's face it, that's true for many adults, too. It's often up to us as parents to help interpret for our kids what's going on in their hearts.

That one episode didn't end the surliness, that's for sure. But scenes like it have lessened the luster and the frequency of the surly-girl routine for my daughter.

That's what it means to me to be on the side of my child.

I'm talking about a coach who makes his team drill much harder to learn the plays because he so wants them to win the game. I'm talking about a teacher who sits with a student and works with him until he really learns the skill at hand, because anything less will not serve that child well. I'm talking about the sergeant who demands and commands respect from his troops because he knows that training will be the difference between life and death in the heat of battle.

I'm a Work in Progress, Too

One fall day I blew it, really blew it. I had all four kids with me at the pumpkin patch. I had paid the entrance fee to get in, but then I felt that I had been misled on what the fee covered. When the manager I complained to wouldn't give me my money back, I started to get angry. Then she got angry. Pretty soon I'd lost it, and we were yelling at each other.

Picture a mother having a meltdown in a pumpkin patch. Not a pretty sight. My children were embarrassed (mortified, actually). Other customers were embarrassed. My emotions completely ruled my response. I was furious, I knew I was right, and *I had to have my way.* The manager finally gave me my money back, letting me know that it was just fine with her that we were leaving.

Let's be clear here. I'm not talking about "losing it" in the basement of United Airlines for misplacing my luggage. I'm not talking about "losing it" at a car dealership for making me wait two hours for a response to an offer price. I'm not talking about "losing it" at the phone company for keeping me home all day waiting for them when they didn't show up. Not that any of these scenarios would have been okay either, but I "lost it" at the pumpkin patch with a bunch of kids.

Ouch.

If I had calmly approached the matter from the beginning, how different it might have been. If I had matter-of-factly stated my case, maybe that manager would have responded differently. Or maybe not.

Maybe I was right. Or maybe not. But just for a few bucks, because I had to have the last word, because I had to be right, I let the encounter become all about me and upset and embarrassed other people, especially my kids.

Within a few minutes, all I felt was remorse. I told my children, now looking for pumpkins at another patch (with much smaller pumpkins, they let me know), how sorry I was for creating a scene. Whether I was right didn't matter. I had let my passions rule me. I had hurt my kids and I had set a terrible example for them.

Later, I dropped them off at home and went to get my nails done and calm down. (Never underestimate the therapeutic benefits of a manicure.) Then I went back to the pumpkin patch and apologized to the manager for my behavior.

Finally, I had another talk with my children. Although this was probably the worst blowup they'd seen me have in public, I'm sorry to say it wasn't the only time I've let myself show, ahem, irritation when I shouldn't have. I told them that I had caused myself and other people, especially them, grief. At age forty, I had acted like a spoiled two-year-old. I asked them to forgive me.

Then I talked to them about training. I told them that when I discipline them and tell them they can't behave a certain way because they have to think about other people first, this is what I'm talking about. When I tell them they can't just vent their feelings, that it's not all about them, this is what I mean. That when I wrestle with them, correct them, and encourage them now, when they are little, to behave responsibly and care for others, I am doing it for a purpose: I hope that all this training will help them develop proper habits of the heart.

It's not just that I don't want my kids yelling at a manager in a pumpkin patch someday, although I suppose that's a start. I want them to develop heart habits that will save them from far more destructive behavior.

That's what it means to be on the side of our children.

I promised my kids I would work to do better and, since then, I largely have, I think, which is an encouragement to them, too. But the "pumpkin patch incident" will live on in our family lore. "Uh-oh, Mom, we're passing that pumpkin patch. Put your heads down, everybody!" When one of them seems to be heading down that path, I can say, "Let's not have a pumpkin patch incident." They know exactly what I mean, and often it turns tears into laughter.

Back to my daughter with the surly-girl habit. Is it possible that she's heard an inappropriate edge in my voice, even when I'm far short of a pumpkin patch–level blowup, that influences her? You bet. I don't think we parents have to self-flagellate, but we do have to be honest with ourselves. It's not fun to see our children reflecting our character flaws back to us, but when they do, we have to face them head-on. We have to persevere. I've told my kids that I'm sorry when I see them imitating my bad habits or the weak parts of my character. I also tell them that while I'll never be perfect, I'm working on those areas, too.

I let my kids know that I'm a work in progress. I'm always trying to do better, and I want them to be works in progress, too. I want them to believe that whether it's their piano skills or their character, whether they are one or one hundred years old, they can always improve. They should never rest where they are right now. None of us should. So whether my daughter got her surly-girl habit from me, from the girls at school, or from the natural tendencies of her own heart, she (and we) can always be striving to change for the better.

The flip side of this is encouragement. When I know my child, I know where she most needs lifting up. When Victoria has had a great attitude, or Peter has handled a difficult task at school without getting frustrated, or Madeleine has been particularly generous to her little sister, or Olivia has consistently obeyed, I let them know that I think they're doing a good job and that I appreciate it. That's part of being on their side, too.

Whose Side Are We On?

The book *Proactive Parenting: Guiding Your Child from Two to Six,* written by faculty members at the Tufts University Eliot-Pearson Department of Child Development, reads like a primer for the parenting culture. The dust jacket proposes that "both child *and parent* [emphasis in the original] are learners as they grow together." Further, the authors maintain that their theme is one of "parents as conductors of their family orchestra."

That analogy might work, I suppose, if children came into the world knowing how to play their instruments beautifully; if they could read and follow the music; if they understood, or could figure out, where and how to improve as musicians; if they could rightly interpret their failures and learn from them, and if they had the natural discipline and inclination to obey the maestro's directions without question, even when they disagreed with him. But how successful would that conductor be if she was presented with "musicians" who had never picked up an instrument?

It upsets some people to think that parents have, by their very position, authority in their children's lives. Perhaps these people wrongly equate "a position of authority" with "absolute authority." In any event, our culture doesn't really like the idea of authority at all. Maybe we're worried that if we admit that parents have authority over their children, this implies that perhaps other relationships that involve authority also must be respected. Apparently that's a problem.

I'm not talking about ordering a pizza, or picking a movie, or even deciding where to go on vacation—compromises can be sought and found in all of these. I'm talking about the basic moral purpose and direction of a child and a family. For this, children must look to their parents for leadership. If parents don't have authority (in spite of our faults and shortcomings), then what's the point of parents at all? Why have or be a parent if an older friend or cheerleader could do the job just fine?

In her excellent book *Ready or Not,* sociologist Kay Hymowitz explores in-depth the strange phenomenon—and the terrible effects—of a culture that no longer fundamentally accepts the premise that parents have authority simply because they are parents, nor really believes any longer that the adult generation has accumulated wisdom from which the young must benefit if they are going to play a truly positive role in society some day. She sees this trend as a danger, and she calls it "anti-culturalism." I call it senseless.

We submit willingly in the grocery store to the anonymous directions of "Eight items or less in this lane," but we don't like it when the boss tells us we need to redo our project by Monday. The closer the relationship, the more we seem to resent the idea of authority within it. For some people, the idea of an authority structure within a family is downright scary. But that thinking results in parents who can never really be on the side of their child.

Consider an umpire in a baseball game whose job is to call the plays at first base. Sometimes he's wrong. A team's manager may shake his fist and complain vociferously, but baseball has no replays. Both teams have to accept the umpire's rulings, regardless of how unfair they think a ruling may be. The integrity of the game, the very *existence* of the game, depends on that umpire's ruling being respected. Imagine the New York Yankees saying, "We don't like the ruling, so we're taking our bats and balls and going home." That would be the end of baseball.

My analogy is not perfect. An umpire is a skilled professional who must prove his qualifications, while anyone who can have or adopt or foster a baby can be a parent. On the other hand, it's highly unlikely that the umpire loves the players enough to lay down his life for them.

Still, the analogy is useful. If the umpire continually makes egregious calls, he will soon find himself fired. But that's not likely, because he at least loves the game itself, he knows it inside and out, and he understands the responsibility he's been given. He is not infallible, but he is integral to the game. His rulings must be respected, even when he makes mistakes, if the players and the game are to exist at all, much less thrive.

The Infallible Parent? No Way!

So it is with parents. And probably no one knows better than we do just how fallible we are. (And when parents have been abusive or neglectful and the situation cannot be corrected, they may rightly be forced to forfeit that position.)

Still, I am encouraging parents to consciously accept what many of us innately grasp, even if we're not sure it's socially acceptable: that they have authority simply because they are parents.

Dr. William Sears, the reigning parenting expert, is the author of many books and columns. I think he has good things to say, but I also think he's wrong when he argues in *The Successful Child* that parents have to "earn" their authority. He writes, "You may be surprised to discover that being a trusted authority figure does not come automatically with the title of parents. Authority has to be earned, even when you're a full-grown adult and your child is an eight-pound newborn."

He's right in the sense that we can't force our children to respect us. But I would argue that one of the best ways to win our children's respect is to properly, and lovingly, assert the authority that comes with our position as parents. Conversely, parents could easily find themselves paralyzed wondering if they'd done the right things that day to earn their authority over their children. That's a good way to lose a child's respect.

Anyway, imagine being pulled over by a police officer while speeding down the street. Do we ask him if he's earned the authority that day to pull us over? I wouldn't recommend trying it. Regardless of that police officer's personal character traits, whatever we may think about her, she has the right to issue a ticket. We wouldn't have very safe streets if it were up to each one of us to decide which police officers had authority and which didn't.

A parent who understands that he has authority because he's the parent has the confidence to use that authority for his child's good *and* to show his child that it's for his good. When we believe we've been given a precious and valuable gift, our children, when we cherish that gift and understand the responsibility that goes along with it, we are much more likely to treat that responsibility carefully.

Even putting aside our moral authority, let's not underestimate the importance of the fact that we simply know more than our kids do. We have experience they don't. We are wiser than they are, and, well, we are more civilized than they are. They desperately need our guidance! Giving it to them is one way to convince them we are on their side.

Think about your relationship with your boss. If you believe that she's out to get you, you'll resent her every instruction. But if you believe that your boss's goal is to encourage you because she wants you to get a promotion in six months, you may welcome those very same instructions, even when they are difficult, because you know she's on your side.

What a difference that perspective makes.

If we can help our kids see that we're on their side, our efforts to train and encourage their characters will be more successful in the long term, because we've reached not just their behavior but their hearts. This will be true even when they can't understand how our actions are in their interest, even when they resist us in the short term.

Look at it this way: if we could parent our kids perfectly—whatever that means—we still wouldn't be guaranteed perfect children! All we can do is persevere in attempting to reach and shape their hearts for the good.

Will we accept our task? We need to believe that rather than being on a journey together—equally helping and teaching one another along the way, as many experts would have us believe—we are on a rescue mission for our kids. We must believe that, rather than just manipulating their behavior, we need to help reach and shape the very hearts of our children. To help that heart learn to delight in the good. We need to understand that our kids need us to understand our mission in their lives. That is what it means to be on the side of our children.

The Cost of Being on Our Children's Side

Finally, we have to understand the cost. I don't mean the dollars-and-cents cost of raising our kids, or even hours on a clock. I mean the personal cost of investing in their lives. The cost of getting to know them intimately, of understanding their strengths and their faults.

There's a cost to recognizing and pursuing our rescue mission in their lives, even when the parenting culture tells us to back off. There's a cost to wrestling with our children, even when the parenting culture tells us to disengage. There's a cost to sticking with what we know is right for our kids, even when—*especially* when—it's not bearing fruit now and might not for a long time.

I mean the cost of persevering.

We can help our kids to believe we are on their side by believing it ourselves. If that's what we hold true in our hearts, we will communicate it to them in our actions.

I've discovered that even when my kids don't believe I'm on their side at that moment, they know *I* believe it. And that makes a huge difference for the better in our relationship.

I don't know exactly what being on your child's side will look like in your home. But I do know it's crucial for the success of all of our homes.

Parenting Check

When there's difficulty with my kids, I sometimes find myself going over to my children's side, instead of going through the work of trying to bring them over to mine, because it's just the easiest way at the moment to avoid conflict. Hey, it happens, and we all survive it. I guess we parents have to ask ourselves, is avoiding conflict with our child the rule of our home? And if it is, how might that undermine our rescue mission for their hearts?

4

It's All About Me — Not!

When my son Peter was in third grade, he and his classmates were given an assignment: create an "All About Me" poster. The instructions were to first cover a big piece of poster board with photos of themselves engaged in their favorite activities. After that, the students were to find pictures in magazines and newspapers that described their interests, cut them out, and glue them to the poster. Next, they were to write bold, positive words about themselves on what was quickly becoming a billboard. Finally, the students were to decorate the poster in an attention-grabbing way.

Neon lights might have been appropriate, because the end product was meant to be a great big advertisement for the student—and only the student—to show why he or she is such a great kid. Right now. As is.

Although Pete could include a picture of his siblings, students were not asked to emphasize anyone or anything other than themselves—not family, not friends, not their responsibilities to the world, not how they could help others, not what they wanted to learn from their teachers, not skills or aspects of their character they wanted to improve, not what they wanted to accomplish. Nope. The theme of Pete's poster was "I'm Peter Hart, and I'm just great on my own."

That's a picture of today's "it's all about me" child.

What made me cringe most about Peter's assignment was how thoroughly it reflected our culture. A culture that teaches even the littlest kids to live with an "all about me" attitude every day. There's no sense of context that includes the child's connection with and responsibilities to his world. The key message is, "You are great, no matter what you do or don't do." And that's scary.

Don't get me wrong. My kids know they are cherished and loved unconditionally, not because they're good kids or only when they're good kids, but simply because they are my children. However, when my kids mess up, I let them know it, I help them do better, and I convince them that I still love them. In contrast, when the neighbor kids mess up, I just send them home.

For the record, I like the neighbors' kids, too, and I very much feel a responsibility to them. I'm good at handing them a treat, for instance, and saying "Thank you, Mrs. Hart" if they don't, and so on. I hope my neighbors do the same when my kids are in their homes. Once when Peter was about four, he observed a neighbor child of his age playing at our house and repeatedly ignoring me as I spoke to him. Peter went over to the little guy and in a stern voice sort of warned him, "I really think you need to listen to my mom and do what she says!"

In any event, little egos absorb this "all about me" message quite instinctively. Far from being the fragile hothouse flowers some experts would like us to believe, those egos flourish naturally. Especially as our society exalts and nurtures a child's self-esteem to the exclusion of all else. No wonder so many miserable kids—and later adults—literally think the world really does revolve around them.

When I was three years old, I took a nap every afternoon. I was the youngest of five children—of *course* my mother put me down for a nap every day, whether I needed it or not. Each afternoon, when I awoke from my nap, I noticed that the same thing happened: the sun would eventually go down and night would come. Some days, this happened soon after my nap. Other days, it happened much later, but, amazingly, it happened over and over again without fail. I came to the obvious conclusion that I was causing the sun to go down each day. (Yes, I'm serious.)

By causing the sunset, it occurred to me, I was ending my playtime. Who wants that? I vividly remember developing a brilliant plan: I would simply do my best to stay awake during naptime and avert the coming of night. Voilà!

Flash: I stayed awake, and night still came.

I was a child who truly believed that my world revolved around me. Literally or figuratively, most very young children go through this stage. It's normal. What is not normal, however, is the way today's parents and the parenting culture seem to encourage children to indulge in this fantasy throughout their development.

I eventually came to realize that I was not responsible for the rising and setting of the sun, and I don't remember feeling any undue personal anxiety over that discovery. But what if I hadn't caught on until I was thirty? That might have had some serious repercussions for my psyche.

One for All . . .

Even a seemingly innocuous activity can promote the "all about me" culture. I keep a running scrapbook of my family and our activities. Creative Memories is probably the best known of the many programs devoted to scrapbooking, with its colorful cutouts, stickers, and page-decorating ideas. My scrapbooks tell the ongoing story of my family's life. I love making them. Much of the year, my dining room table is strewn with materials, photos, papers, and glue sticks for my "picture books," as my girls call them.

The Creative Memories program encourages moms (since they're the ones usually making the scrapbooks) to create a family book *and* a separate book for each child, focusing on that little one's life, activities, and accomplishments. This is not entirely so the Creative Memories folks can sell more material; it's so each child can have his or her own picture book.

When my Creative Memories consultant—who is terrific, by the way—encouraged me to start individual books for each of my kids, my response was, "Not a chance!" With four kids, I no more have time to make individual scrapbooks than I have time to go into NASA's astronaut program. But I had another reason, too. I did not want take my children's childhood years out of the context of our family life.

I have individual pictures of my kids all over my house, in addition to the group photos. Each one of my kids is unique, and I hardly think making a scrapbook for a child is going to do permanent damage to their little psyches. I have one myself from when I was little. It's basically a montage of my annual posed photos, but considering I was the youngest of five, that's saying quite something about my mom that she did that for me. And, yes, it's pretty neat.

So if anybody reading this wants to make individual scrapbooks for each of their kids, go for it. All I'm saying is that for my family, already full of children who are convinced the world does or should revolve around them, I decided it would be a good idea to keep only family scrapbooks in order to emphasize our family life.

What I mean by that is that what my children accomplish and learn and celebrate during their growing-up years is wonderful—and it's part of the fabric of our life together. It springs from the rootedness and encouragement of the whole family. I was afraid that for my kids, a "story of your life" book that focused on the individual, and in which the rest of the family was essentially background noise, would just make it too easy for them ignore the fundamental family context of their lives. Who they are comes from the history of who *we* are, and that's what I want to reinforce.

Though my kids might sometimes think otherwise, in my family my children are—blessedly—*not* on their own.

Sure, as I create my picture books, I might focus on an individual's activities. One page might be about my son's Cub Scout troop meeting with President Bush, and another might highlight my daughter's school musical. More typically, however, a page focuses on all of us on summer vacation or at the fall festival. The point is that even individual triumphs, which I'm happy to acknowledge and celebrate, fall within the larger context of our family—its growth and connectedness and story. Instead of his or her own scrapbook, each child will eventually get a copy of the family album. But of course individual scrapbooks are not really the issue here. The issue is creating an environment that counterbalances "all about me."

How High Should I Jump?

And "it's all about me" children are everywhere. I regularly see kids (yes, too often including my own) interrupting their parents or expecting their parents to drop everything when they call, "Look at me, Mom!" That's not surprising. What is distressing is that too many parents seem to respond "How high?" when their kids say "Jump!"

Conversely, I also see surly, angry, disconnected teens, rolling their eyes at their utterly terrified parents, with whom they seem to want no connection.

Today's parents are likely to accede to their child's demands—to interrupt, to be the center of attention, or to be left completely alone—whenever and as the child stipulates.

Cowed by their children, these parents don't make the connection between fostering the "all about me" attitude and their current despair. At best, as I have heard too many parents complain, "Gee, we just can't have a conversation with our friends when the kids are around," or "I can't get two words out of my teen."

We've all been in an adult gathering on which some child rushes in and the adults, often not just the child's own parents, are expected to drop everything and focus on the little one. Typically, Mom and Dad might be led away by the child to go look at or do whatever the child wants them to. That's when I roll my eyes. (I'm hardly saying my kids never try to boss me around—nor am I saying I never give in—sigh. In fact, it happens enough that I've said to each of them at some point, "I'm sorry, dear, did I not say 'how high' fast enough when you ordered me to jump?")

In contrast, how often have you heard an adult say to a little one, "No, dear, you may not interrupt us. I'm chatting with the adults right now, and when I'm done I'll come see what you are up to. Now go play"?

Not often enough.

What happens when these kids grow up? A reader of one of my columns who sees this attitude firsthand wrote:

> I am in a business that hires a lot of young folks . . . teenagers and young adults. I'm constantly amazed at the incredibly self-centered, self-important, egomaniacal attitude of almost every single one of these people. The hardworking, truly intelligent, and conscientious youngster is about as rare as a precious diamond. This includes those clear into their thirties. *And* they are always bored and unhappy.

Hey, friend, don't sugarcoat it!

Let's Hear It for the Home Team

So what's the antidote for "it's all about me" kids? It starts with finding ways large and small to teach them it's *not* all about them.

One family I know has a "family cup." It started when their children were young and has continued even though they're all adults now. Whenever there is rejoicing in their extended family—a new child, a job promotion, a new home, a milestone birthday—that family member is awarded the family cup. (Literally an inexpensive trophy bought decades ago.) For whoever holds the cup, it's a reminder that their joy or their achievement is not just about them, but is shared and cheered by an extended family. As the cup is given to the next family member with something to celebrate, there is a sharing of the new source of joy. Given the size of the family, it's far more likely that at any time the family members are celebrating someone else, not themselves. What a wonderful habit for the heart, and how wonderful to learn to have so many sources of happiness to celebrate.

Another mom of a teenager has gotten into the habit of drawing a stick person in the air with her finger whenever her daughter whines too much about something going wrong in her pretty delightful life. I don't know how mom and daughter came to an understanding on the symbolism, but it means, "Honey, it's not all about you."

I know several families that make a practice out of volunteering together in their community, or whose teens go to do short-term mission trips in other countries during the summer months. That's a great way to open our kids' eyes to a world of "other."

One way my family tries to combat the "it's all about me" culture is to emphasize the "Hart Team." In that way, my children see themselves as rooted in and responsible to something larger than themselves—their family.

Many folks pay lip service to the importance of family. But too often, family seems to be a group of autonomous individuals sharing little more than an address. When I stress the Hart Team, I emphasize working together to achieve goals and making it a priority to care about each member of the team, taking particular care of the littlest ones or the ones most in need at any given time. We're not competing with other "teams," we're simply trying to work together to be the best "team" that we can be. We rejoice when something good happens to one of us and share the burden when someone is having a rough day—at least we try to. We talk about how the Hart Team is for life.

This is harder now that the Hart Team looks different, no doubt, but the principle remains the same. I want my family to pull together. If my children are screaming at one another, tormenting one another, or insisting that life is not fair because they are not getting as much of something as a sibling did—or otherwise having a typical day—I just know I have to persevere all the more in promoting the Hart Team. I find myself saying things like, "Come on, kids. The Hart Team doesn't quit." Or "The Hart Team doesn't speak unkindly about its members." Or "The Hart Team doesn't exclude a member from play."

Yes, it's corny—but let's not underestimate corny. It can make you feel pretty darn good. I find the kids really identify with the team concept, that sometimes the team gets their attention when other things don't. That's because I'm convinced that deep down, in spite of the culture, we all like to feel we're connected to something bigger than just us.

The team concept makes the family concept more concrete, and the kids love it—most of the time. Okay, much of the time.

One year at a fall festival on a big country farm, Ben and I signed up to do the corn maze. Four kids, stroller and all. Wouldn't that be fun? How tough could it be? The sun was beginning to set when we figured out it could be horrifically tough. We were an hour and a half and who knows how far into a six-foot-high maze. We'd had it. We were done. We finally broke through one of the walls of corn to blessed release. Freedom.

Peter was horrified. "Mom and Dad," he wailed, "you said the Hart Team never quits!" Almost in unison, Ben and I said, "Pete, we didn't quit. We lost!" The team doesn't have to be perfect.

The Best-Laid Plans . . .

There are lots of great ways to reinforce your family. Almost anything you do together counts. I know some families who take tae kwon do together. Other families set aside every Friday night, or every other Friday night, for a fun family activity. One week that might be a movie. Another week it might be a game of laser tag. In every case, it's a family doing something together—and it's a priority.

This might become complicated as the children grow older—jobs, school activities, and friends need to be navigated. Even now it's so easy for me to let other responsibilities creep in on family time. I have to constantly be on guard against letting outside things interfere, while not panicking that family life will be lost forever if the kids and I can't get a fun activity in some weekends. Even some weekends in a row. We will survive. Still, it's a habit, a mindset really, that successful families maintain as long as the children live at home.

Family trips are a great way to break away together, but I've found that family trips can make some parents really nervous. What if, after all that planning and expense, the trip doesn't live up to expectations? Well, so what?

In 2001, even before the horrific terrorist attacks, Ben and I considered driving our family from the East Coast to the Chicago area for

Thanksgiving. After those attacks, I wasn't getting on a plane—and neither were my kids. It was car travel for us. We had it all planned. Our goal was to leave at 5:00 a.m. the Tuesday before Thanksgiving. We would pack all four of our sweet little sleeping bundles into their seats, buying us about three hours of peace and quiet. We had visions of the kids blissfully snoozing while we sipped rich, fresh coffee with lots of cream from a high-tech thermos. We'd watch the sun come up and have thoughtful discussions about our family life.

Well, we finally departed about 7:30 a.m. in the pouring rain. The kids were wide awake and had been bouncing around since 5:30. We forgot the coffee in the rush, and our intimate discussions centered on who was to blame for getting out the door so late, putting us in the thick of rush-hour traffic.

And that was the best part of the trip.

Only fifteen minutes into our journey, just after we'd gotten onto the interstate, we heard banging above us. Ben and I agreed that we'd better check the roof rack at the next exit. No need—seconds later, the soft vinyl bag filled with children's clothes ripped free of its straps on the roof rack, becoming a projectile launched onto the highway. (Mercifully, no one was hurt.)

Complete shock descended. Ben pulled over and actually backed up in the emergency lane. Too much time and money were tied up in those little wardrobes to just leave the bag on the highway. To our dismay, we quickly discovered that the bag had ripped open, strewing children's clothes across three lanes of traffic.

I am not making this up: in the rain, during rush hour, Ben stopped the cars that had already slowed. With one hand holding up traffic, he gingerly reached out with the other for a piece of underwear here, a pair of khakis there. I made sure the children were buckled in safely and joined him. Even at the time, I wondered why we weren't being honked at mercilessly. It quickly became obvious—the drivers observing the scene were doubled over in such hysterical laughter that they weren't able to curse us.

My focus was shoes. I wasn't leaving before I found my son's new loafers or that second little patent leather mary jane. My favorite pullover for my middle daughter was three lanes out into the highway. I snatched it. (To this day Olivia still wears it.) A highway safety crewman finally arrived to assist us. I hoped he would comfort us by saying he'd seen this before. He didn't. We piled the wet clothes onto our crying children so we could exit the scene before perishing from embarrassment.

I've always wondered if we made the morning traffic report that day.

The car trip didn't get any worse after that, but it didn't get any better either. We had borrowed a TV/VCR for the trip, but it wasn't the salvation we thought it would be. The driver and front passenger can't see the movie but, without earphones, they can't escape it either. We listened to the "Oompa Loompa" song from *Willy Wonka & the Chocolate Factory* about fifty times. I started noticing the planes overhead—and thinking how lucky those passengers were.

That trip didn't live up to our original expectations, but in the end it wildly exceeded them. It was the most miserable and the most wonderful time I can remember. I'll never again worry about something not going right on one of our family outings. That adventure remains the most talked-about trip we've ever taken. It was far from perfect, but we handled adversity together. I hear many families talk of their best trips being the ones with the leaky cabin roofs, the car without air-conditioning, the change of plans because of the hurricane. Don't worry—just enjoy it together. And remember to laugh.

Something else our family does is the "appreciation game." We sit around, usually before bed, and take turns discussing what we appreciate about someone else in the family. Sometimes it doesn't go quite the way I'd planned. One child might say of another, "I appreciate when

Peter only bothers me most of the day and not all day." But usually the kids take it pretty seriously. I'll even hear one child appreciating another in a way I wouldn't have imagined, for instance, "I appreciate that Madeleine made me laugh when I was sad today." That's another way to get our kids to focus on and appreciate and celebrate others, and to perhaps combat the "all about me" culture.

"The World Doesn't Revolve Around You"

Hey, let's be clear. Plenty of times my children still think that if the world doesn't revolve around them, it darn well should! I myself need to work daily to overcome this natural tendency of the human heart, in my own life.

I take comfort in the fact that at least I know what I'm aiming for. I know what is at stake. I am, after all, on a rescue mission for my children's hearts.

Many times, I've reminded myself of that rescue mission as I say to my kids, "This is not all about you, dear." Though the elites of the parenting culture might cringe to hear it, I've said to each of my children at one time or another, "You can't (or you must) do this, have that, or act such and such a way because this family does not revolve around you. There are other members you need to consider. And you have responsibilities to them." Or perhaps, after a child has lamented some disappointment, even a legitimate one, long enough, "You just do not have the right to make other people miserable over your unhappiness, honey." At other times, I might tell one child, "I can't focus on you right now, dear. I'm focusing on your sister and her needs at the moment."

I'm not afraid to tell my children that they can't interrupt adults. As in, "No, honey, you can't barge in and tell us everything about the movie you just saw—in real time. We're talking with Papa right now and you need to sit still and listen to him." Or even, "The adults are talking, honey. Go play outside. This is the grown-up zone."

When my daughter complained about not being able to go to a birthday party because we were going to be out of town, for instance, I didn't join her pity party. For one thing, little ones these days log about 15,786 birthday parties during their youth. For another, I told her that the best decision for the family was to take the trip we'd planned. I told her I was sorry she'd miss this party (and I really was) and only get to go to 15,785 other parties during her childhood, but after a relatively short mourning period, she had to stop complaining about it. I reminded her of her responsibility to be a good sport and set an example, particularly for her younger siblings, even if she didn't feel like it at the moment. Her calling to do the right thing trumped her right to feel sorry for herself. She survived both missing the party and not being able to make everyone else miserable about it.

Before the parenting culture collectively winces and shudders, I hope they ask themselves this: Which child is better off? The one who's allowed to wallow in her self-righteous indignation and grief over the missed party, tormenting others as well as herself? Or the child who is told she must move on—and does?

That's not to say there aren't times when children's real needs, as opposed to their felt needs, do require accommodation. A young child's need for a nap or an older child's chance to participate in an important sports event might dictate the family's schedule at the moment. Mom and Dad come in handy by helping a child distinguish between his perceived needs—which won't always be met—and his real needs. Having a family that accommodates one another is one way a child avoids becoming an "all about me" kid.

Most kids, I think, feel incredible relief to learn that the world, even their world, does not revolve around them. Those who continue to believe into adulthood that the world is "all about me" are headed for trouble.

I would ask parents who are convinced that it's all right to allow the child to be the center of the family's universe, to receive attention whenever she asks for it—to believe it's "all about her"—to think about this: Somewhere out there, other parents are raising your child's future spouse. Is this how you hope they're doing it?

Of course, our children are individuals, with unique gifts and personalities and challenges, and they need different kinds of care and recognition. One of the best ways to appropriately nourish, encourage, and respond to those little individuals may be to teach them that it's not all about them—by grounding them in the so-important notion of "other."

Parenting Check

It's very easy for us parents to get carried away with our own kids and to let them become the center of the family universe. There's nothing wrong with responding "That's great" when a child says, "Watch me, Mom!" That's part of the fun of being a parent. The question is, do the children and their perceived needs, including their perceived needs at the moment, such as their need for attention, rule the home? How do we feel about communicating to them, "I love you, but neither the world nor this family revolves around what you *think* your needs are at this instant"?

I also think the family team concept is important, however that looks in any one person's home. It's worth considering how we can advance that concept in our own homes. The family cup? The appreciation game? What might work (and what might not work) for you?

5

Our Children, Our Idols

It gets worse. "It's all about me" kids are almost always idolized kids.

When I was pregnant with my second child, I was on a news program with a so-called child advocate. During a break, she asked me about the impending birth. I had a suspicion about child advocates, so I decided to be mischievous: I told her it was my second child and that my husband and I were excited to be one-third of the way toward our goal of six.

She was openly horrified with that answer. "Six!" she almost snarled. "How will you ever give them individual attention?" Her disgust hung in the air. "I don't know," I replied, "I suppose they'll give each other attention."

The child advocate did not approve of this answer. I suspect she wasn't as much of a child advocate as she was an advocate of idolizing kids.

Dr. Patricia Dalton is a clinical psychologist and mother of three grown kids. In a 2002 *Washington Post* column, she described the phenomenon of what she calls "über-parents."

> They decorate their children's rooms in stimulating colors, buy educational toys, forgo playpens and give baby massages. They space their children according to the best advice of child-development experts. They sign their kids up for . . . gymnastics classes and apply to the most progressive preschools and enroll them in soccer at age four. They sacrifice personal time, friendships and their own interests—sometimes even their sex lives. They let their kids interrupt them and drop everything to take advantage of every teaching moment. And perhaps most important, they take every opportunity to build up their children's self-esteem.

Dalton says that children of über-parents end up in her practice because, as adults, they don't want to leave the family nest. Why on earth would they want to go? Their parents certainly don't make them, and it's awfully comfy there. Dalton says she is seeing more deeply entangled, conflicted, and difficult parent–adult child relationships.

Dalton suggests that families that were not so child-focused were probably happier. They certainly raised kids with more generous spirits. In contrast, today's children of overindulgent parents, she says, "are takers, not doers or givers."

It's hard to imagine how such children will find joy in life.

If You Want Sympathy, Look It Up in the Dictionary

Just as Dalton describes it, parents like mine used to actually say things like, "Don't bother me unless you are bleeding," and "If you want sympathy, look it up in the dictionary." My own parents would take us kids to the homes of their friends for parties and gatherings—and it would never occur to any of us to have the children mix with the adults. We'd hang out with the other kids, the adults with the adults, and everyone would have a good time.

Nor do I remember sharing any angst with my mom about my sundown fantasy being blown to bits. What does stand out is this: she loved my siblings and me passionately. She and I were very close until her death in 1995. She really was my best friend. Even when I was a teenager, I thought she was pretty awesome, and we got along well.

But I also don't remember her ever taking me to the park—although I think she played the Candy Land game with me one time. I just don't think it would have crossed my mind to ask her to do such things. That's what friends and all those brothers and my sister were there for. (I do remember my siblings asking, "Mom, do we have to take Betsy?" "Yesssss!" would come the reply from who knows where in the house.)

My pals and I played for hours without trying to pull our parents into our fun. It would have seemed silly to us to have tried to include them.

Yes, I know, in some ways it's harder today. We feel that our kids can't go to parks by themselves like we did. (But then again, even some of those fears may be wildly overblown. If you ask the average person on the street how many children are abducted in the United States by strangers every year, he'd probably say tens of thousands. The real answer, according to the Justice Department, was 115 in 2002—the most recent year for which data is available—and that's pretty typical because most children are abducted by family members. As parents today, we're typically fearful even when the risk of danger is small.)

I'm hardly saying kids have to be put in harm's way to play by themselves. It is true that when I was little, my mother would quite literally tell us to go play in the street. We had a fairly quiet road in front of our home on which we would play hopscotch, four-square, you name it. When a car came, we would just get out of the way until it passed, and then go back to our play. I would *never* allow my children to play like that today. But I might send them to the basement, or a side yard, or even the park just down the street from where we live in order to play *on their own*.

So, what about my dad? For starters, I don't remember him attending even one of my birthday parties as a child. I'm not even sure he knew about my birthday parties. I would have fainted with surprise if he'd shown up. But so what? He was crazy about us and we all knew it. He had five little ones to provide for on commissions—how on earth could he be hosting our birthday parties, too?

I do remember him, however, attaching the toboggan to the car on snowy winter nights and piling us and the neighbor kids on it. He'd drive at pretty high speeds on our suburban Chicago streets, particularly around the corners, until we fell off laughing and screaming so hard we could barely breathe. Then we'd run after the car and try to jump on the moving toboggan. Today my dad would be put in jail for reckless endangerment, but that's the kind of cool stuff dads did then and gosh it was fun. Today my dad is eighty, and we are closer than ever. Maybe the toboggan rides, which back then we kids called "screeliching," are part of the reason why.

I digress. The point is that when it came to Dad not showing up at birthday parties, we coped. Today's kids are definitely *not* asked to cope.

I lived at home after I graduated from college—for about nine days. I left for my first job in Washington, D.C., a little more than a week after ending my senior year in college. Mom and Dad had been working the phones to get me working *anywhere*. Goodness knows I wasn't about to make a whole lot of effort in that that direction myself. I was, well, pretty unmotivated. I liked to think I was kind of smart and a lot of fun to be around, but that was about all I had to offer the world. Worse, I actually thought it was more than enough to offer the world.

Fortunately, I had parents who weren't going to allow me to wallow in that misperception for long. To help me get started on this road to life, my dad cosigned a loan, which I was fully responsible for repaying. That was it. "See ya, honey."

One minute, I was wearing sweatpants and pulling all-nighters for finals, loving life at the University of Illinois. What a protected cocoon. It was great! Nine days later, I was 750 miles away, sitting at a desk and answering the phone, getting up earlier than I had in four years, and worrying about paying the rent.

That stunk.

How did this happen, I wondered. Wasn't I supposed to get a summer off to contemplate my navel? Didn't my parents owe me a trip to Europe? I mean, didn't the world revolve around me?

I quickly figured out that no one owed me anything. It had finally hit me—the world really *didn't* revolve around me after all. And this realization came late in spite of all the "right" things my parents did. Imagine if they were like too many of today's parents and encouraged me to think the world *did* revolve around me. (My four older siblings would, of course, make the case that my parents were way too focused on me. I'm not sure whose memories are more accurate—the truth is probably somewhere in the middle.)

In any event, I remember one Friday in those early working days, when I had about $4.50 to my name. That needed to last until Monday's paycheck. I carefully calculated how much I needed to ride public transportation home on Friday and back to work on Monday. It came out to just about $4.50. So in order to just buy milk and cereal for the weekend, I sold all my postage stamps to my office mates. It never occurred to me to ask Mom and Dad to pitch in. Supporting myself was my job now. I made it back to work on Monday with three cents in my pocket—but I made it. I had learned to cope.

In an episode of the brilliant show *Seinfeld* (yes, I think something can be cynical—and hilarious—and still offer worthwhile insights), comedian Jerry Seinfeld is doing a stand-up routine. It goes something like this: "Have you ever heard a guy say, 'Boy, things are going well for me. I got a promotion at work, my bowling score is going way up—and next month, if things continue to go this well, I'm going to move in with my parents!'" The television audience erupts into laughter, because even as recently as the 1990s when that show aired, for an adult to return to his parents' home to live was equated, right or wrong, well, with the term "loser."

Contrast that with a *Time* cover story, in January 2005, "They Just Won't Grow Up." *Time* tells us how young people between ages twenty-two and twenty-six or so, people once called adults, are now called "the Twixters." They live with their parents in astoundingly high numbers. Today fully 20 percent of all American twenty-six-year-olds are living with Mom and Dad. (That's twice the rate of 1970.) They hop from "job to job and date to date." Most typically, they are living rent-free or are heavily subsidized by their parents.

One insightful Twixter told *Time*, "I do not want to be a parent. I mean, hell, why would I?" Why in the world should they, indeed? This fellow and his friends are having too much fun being kids. And their parents are encouraging them in their extended adolescence.

According to *Time* the Twixters are spending heavily on everything from new cars to flat-screen TVs. The Twixters have money—they just want to spend it on the "fun" stuff. Forget working hard, saving, sacrificing. For these young adults, it's too often about "me" and "now." Over and over the Twixters reported to *Time* that they didn't want any responsibilities in life. They are too busy having a good time. But here's the problem: if we as a culture don't encourage young adults to grow up and embrace real responsibilities, both for themselves and especially to others, we rob them of the chance to become tangibly connected to the web of the community around them, to become part of something bigger than just themselves at a crucially important time in their lives.

An "all about me" world can, in the end, be pretty lonely.

Hey, it's wonderful to have fun. But there's a difference between an adult having fun being an adult, having all the joy and sorrow and pain and just living that comes with growing up—and an adult having fun by pretending to be a child. Something is very wrong with the latter, because it's not good enough to live like that if we want to live fully. But this, sadly, is what can come from being an idolized child.

Here's what another reader, a high-school teacher, wrote to me about these "all about me" idolized kids:

> Each day, I see young people who have not a clue as to the skills and attitudes they are going to need as they progress through the "real world." Many students believe that their grades should be based upon the fact that they merely breathe enough air in my classroom over a specified amount of time. . . . We have pumped our young people full of self-importance in the hope that this would transfer to their acceptance of the importance of others; yet, we have created nothing more than a generation of selfish and rude people who truly believe that they are the sun around which all else revolves.

This is what happens when kids don't figure out early that they aren't responsible for the coming of nightfall.

The Blessing of a Skinned Knee

California child psychologist Wendy Mogel relates this common experience counseling parents and children in her wonderful book *The Blessing of a Skinned Knee:* "After conducting tests and telling parents that their child was 'within normal limits,' the parents were frequently disappointed. In their view, a diagnosable problem was better than a normal, natural limitation. A problem can be fixed, but a true limitation requires adjustment of expectations and acceptance of an imperfect son or daughter."

She recounts a school principal telling her, "Too many parents want everything fixed by the time their child is eight. Children develop in fits and starts, but nobody has time for that anymore. No late bloomers, no slow starters, nothing unusual accepted! . . . Not every child has unlimited potential in all areas. . . . Parents just need to relax a little and be patient." But it takes a lot of work to keep an idolized child on that pedestal, so of course these parents can't relax.

There is nothing wrong with stimulating colors and educational toys, with wanting good schools for our kids and wanting them to do their best. But when we obsess about such things, when we're afraid that the wrong music in our child's crib now might keep her out of Harvard later *and ruin her chance at a happy life,* we should start seeing red lights and hearing buzzers.

Pulitzer Prize–winning child psychologist Robert Coles recognized this trend decades ago when he wrote in *Time* magazine in 1975:

> More than the people of any country in the world . . . Americans publicly talk about and worry about their children. We have the overwhelming majority of the world's child psychologists and child psychiatrists. Our universities and, increasingly, our high schools devote themselves to a proliferation of courses in child development. . . . The prevailing concern of parents is not what the child ought to believe and live up to (in the way of standards, rock-bottom beliefs, a religious faith) but what is "best" for the child. . . .
>
> Through him, through her, one can get hold of the future, secure it, possess it, mold it, ensure it. With the decline of religion and an increasing affluence, the happiness, security and welfare of children become

for many a major obsession which, in turn, has a broad and strong impact on the way children look, play, get educated, and, not least, are treated at home.

In fact, for many parents, there is an ironic duality to their family life: on the one hand, a desire that children have the "best." And on the other hand a willingness to turn to others in order to make sure that such an objective is realized. Those others are doctors, teachers, camp counselors, "experts" of various kinds; they are the men and women who, it is hoped, will year by year work on a child, make him or her stronger, sounder, more ambitious, more effective, more competent—better able to get ahead.

I think Coles was describing the tip of the iceberg. When it comes to our kids, parents today are terrified of doing *anything* remotely less than perfectly perfect. That isn't just a big load for the parents to carry—it's a crushing load for a child to bear.

Mogel told me that she thinks the words "special" and "kids" are connected way too often in our culture. As she discusses in her book, parents and kids would be so much happier if Mom and Dad accepted the fact that most of our children are wonderfully ordinary.

Personally, I wonder if one of the reasons for the rise of the über-parents is the decline in large families. Fewer kids means we *can* do more for each one. And the fewer the kids, the more eggs are in each kid's basket. They *have* to succeed—and we have to make sure they do. Yes, I know really messed-up, selfish people exist in families with lots of kids. And I know many wonderful, thoughtful people who were only children. But in my own experience, at least, I find people from large families to be some of the happiest, most easygoing, and least self-obsessed people I know. My personal observation may not count for a lot, but it makes some sense that it would be that way.

I'm guessing that guilt also plays a big part in the idolizing of children. Parents who spend more time away from their kids—pursuing the golden ring of "more stuff"—are less likely to say, "Go outside and play and *do not* come inside until I call you" (a personal favorite of mine). There's no doubt that as religious influence has waned in this country, many parents are trying to fill a void in their spiritual life by vainly putting *everything* into the one thing that will live on after them—their kids. Or maybe we as a culture have simply come to view our pleasure, our contentedness, our happiness, our ease of life as the preeminent good. And if it's good for us, it's good for our children, too—even when it's not really good for either of us.

So, each child is nurtured and protected and fawned over like a hothouse flower, when they are actually hardy little geraniums who need to be outside soaking up the sun. Even if being left out in the sun means they will also get rained on a lot. After all, they need rain to thrive, too.

It's Possible to Give Too Much Attention to Your Kids

I think it is quite possible to give too much attention to your kids. Here's what one über-mom posted on the Internet about her little one. This mom is part of the growing trend of attachment parenting (AP). AP recommends that babies be worn in a sling almost all the time, going everywhere with Mom or Dad. They should be picked up as they wish. There should be a family bed, and the baby should be breast-fed well beyond the first year, often into the second and even third. Their cries, even as they become young children (when some would call their cries

outbursts and tantrums), should be immediately tended to or, preferably, preempted.

This mom writes:

> I am a stay-at-home mom and Demmi spends all her time with me. I am
> rarely away from her . . . I don't want to be! The entire first 1.5 years
> [of her life] I was only away from her for a combined total of 26 hours.
> I only left her when I absolutely had to, and those times she stayed
> only with grandparents, who adore her. Our bond is strong, as na-
> ture intended. This is the way parenting has been since time beyond
> beginning.

(Actually, in the Western world, it's been that way only when circumstances, like poverty, forced it.)

This mom believes it is literally cruel for a child to sleep by himself.
She writes of little ones who sleep in their own cribs or beds as being
"tortured by isolation" and falling asleep only with "broken hearts."
Her rhetoric may be a little extreme, but her thinking is right in line with
mainstream AP philosophy.

This mom spends *all* her time with her daughter? Is that to meet the
girl's needs, or Mom's? I'm just guessing here, but I think that Dad
would love to have had Mom away from the child for more than twenty-
six hours in a year and a half.

This is an idolized child.

I think that if a mom wants to carry her young toddler with her
everywhere, sleep with her, spend all her time with her, and breast-feed
her extensively, that's her business. If that's what she and Dad feel
called to do, then they should go for it with gusto. I'm even fully willing
to admit that this little girl may be a real charmer (though I doubt it has
anything to do with attachment parenting).

The problem is that attachment-parenting advocates make grand claims for their philosophy and believe that all parents should practice it. But their claims just aren't substantiated. They argue that more "connected" kids do better in life. That's true, but there's no evidence that attachment parenting produces more connected kids. If it did, we'd have to argue that entire previous generations of middle-class Americans for whom AP was an unknown concept—those millions of seemingly content, normal people who contributed to their communities, fought the wars, stayed married, loved their families, worked for just social change—went through life being awfully unattached. It just doesn't make sense.

But attachment parenting—including one of its core tenets, that young children should not be allowed to experience frustration—is growing. Whatever the merits of attachment parenting, it seems its increasing popularity is related to more parents putting their children on pedestals. The idea of answering to their children *at every moment* well into childhood fits the purpose of many of these moms and dads. Being an idol may sound like fun, but it has to be an enormous burden. As I asked in the previous chapter, is this how you hope your child's future spouse is being raised?

Don't get me wrong for a minute. We can and should love our children to "Reese's Pieces," as I tell my kids. (I know it makes no sense— that's what makes it fun.) We should delight in them, and believe that without them our lives would be far less meaningful—and less chaotic and heartbreaking and interesting and wonderful. There will be times when we make sacrifices for them. Most obviously, what loving parent wouldn't lay down his life for his child? But that's different from idolizing our children or, to apply one dictionary's definition of that word to our kids, creating for ourselves a false picture of the exalted character of our children and then admiring them to excess.

Irrational Love: All the More Need for Rational Parents

I agree with Urie Bronfenbrenner, professor emeritus of human development at Cornell University, who says, "Each child needs someone to make an irrational commitment to him." How true! As parents, our love for our children *is* irrational. This is most evident in the fact that we love our children more than they will ever love us, and we know it. We love them with a wholeness and abandonment that they cannot understand until they become parents themselves. Most amazingly, not only do we not resent the different "levels" of love between us and our kids, we fully accept that that's the way it *should* be. In what other kind of love would we say, "I love more than I am loved—and that's great"?

But even though our love for our children may be irrational, we parents need to work hard to think straight. We need to realize that, in our culture, we too often idealize and idolize our kids. I'm afraid that not enough moms today would say, "No, not now, dear, Mom's busy," to her child—and not feel guilty about it. That's too bad. I suggest that a lot of kids would benefit greatly if they were told exactly that from time to time. Or maybe, "Go outside and don't come in for an hour," or "Don't interrupt," or "One step closer to this bathroom door, pal, and you're in *big trouble.*" Whatever the language, you get the point. Instead, we've become über-parents who buy Baby Einstein tapes before the baby is conceived. When he does arrive, we let him know it's "all about him."

In May 2001, Lisa Jennings of the Scripps Howard News Service wrote about the addition of the second (and often last) child to a family. She looked at the work of anthropologist Rebecca Upton, who has studied the effect of a second child on the typical middle-class family (often both Mom and Dad work). According to these folks, it's no breeze. One mother described it as overwhelming. Another with girls ages five and three said, "You just don't have any downtime anymore."

My question is, "Why not?"

But most telling was what this mom told Jennings: one of the most difficult aspects of her second child's arrival, she complained, was the lack of time with her firstborn. She was home with the children during the day while her husband worked, but "instead of one-on-one it was one-on-two," she said. "You worry about what the first is feeling." Well, whatever the first is feeling, she's probably a tiny bit closer to getting off the pedestal, at least sometimes, and that's a good thing.

Believe me, I understand that handling even two healthy young kids can make life busy, and they can make a mom really tired. But "overwhelming"? A child who is taught early on to occupy, entertain, or soothe herself is given a great gift. If she's not given that gift, that could be a symptom of a bigger problem: an idolized child who is learning that "it's all about me." And that's a pretty good way to stunt a child's soul.

A friend of mine described a scene she witnessed as she was waiting for her family at the post office: a three- or four-year-old child came out of the post office with her parents and grandparents. She had a toy waddling duck on a stick. The adults cajoled the child to get into the car. "Honey, why don't you walk your duck over to the car?" No way. "C'mon, honey, let's go this way. Wouldn't ducky like to get in the car and go for a nice ride?" At every turn, the child gave an adamant no.

She wasn't screaming or crying or throwing any kind of a tantrum. But she was definitely running the show. Did it ever occur to the adults to pick the little girl up, put her in the backseat, strap her in, and drive off? Apparently not. My friend watched the scene for twenty minutes before she left. Who knows how those parents ever persuaded the child to get in the car? All we know is that what lies ahead for those parents and that little girl probably isn't pretty. This is an idolized child.

Wendy Mogel, in *Blessing*, distills age-old Jewish teaching into these tenets, which, I think, might help to provide an antidote to the idolized child. She encourages parents to:

Accept that your children are both unique and ordinary.
Teach them to honor their parents and to respect others—family, friends, and community.
Teach them to be resilient, self-reliant, and courageous.
Teach them to be grateful for their blessings.
Teach them the value of work.
Teach them to make their table an altar—to approach food with an attitude of moderation, celebration, and sanctification.
Teach them to accept rules and to exercise self-control.
Teach them the preciousness of the present moment.
Teach them about God.

Great stuff.

Parenting Check

If you were the parents of the child who refused to get into the car, what would you have done? Promised to give her a treat if she complied? Threatened her with the removal of a privilege if she didn't?

Can you picture physically picking her up, over her protests if necessary, strapping her into her seat, driving off—and not feeling guilty about it?

We probably all see at least bits and pieces of that idolized child in our own children. We want to please our kids and make their lives comfortable. Let's face it. We're pretty nuts about our kids. And that's great. But we have to realize that we can be irrationally crazy about our children, and still be rationally pursuing our rescue mission for their hearts. And that means getting them off that pedestal.

6

The Self-Delusion of Self-Esteem

I recently sat in a doctor's waiting room with a young mom and her son, who was about two. This little guy literally could not move without being praised to the sky by Mom. If he opened a book, he was so wonderful; if he closed the book, he was so smart. If he sat still for two seconds, he was such a darling, dear little guy who was doing such an awesome job. If he moved, he was so sweet to have moved in just the way he did. All along, Mom understood how hard this all was for him and how he was being incredibly, terrifically, super-good for Mom.

What's this mother going to come up with when her little guy does something that *really* calls for some praise? Conversely, what's going to happen when that little boy is around peers, or other adults, who don't compare his every step with Neil Armstrong's walk on the moon? That kid may be in for some rough times.

We've just looked at the world of "all about me" kids and the "idolized child." These are elements of a larger problem our culture faces:

the "cult of self-esteem." Nowhere is this more evident than in the parenting culture.

I'm Gonna Like Me

Here's what the parenting culture tells us about self-esteem:

"Helping your child grow up with strong self-esteem is the most important task of parenthood."—From the popular (if strangely titled) parenting website positivelymad.co.uk

"Nothing is as important as self-esteem to a child's well-being and success. . . . All children have the right to feel good about themselves exactly as they are."—From *Just Because I Am: A Child's Book of Affirmation*

"[Your child's] attitude toward himself has a direct bearing on how he lives all parts of his life. In fact, *self-esteem is the mainspring that slates every child for success or failure as a human being*" (emphasis in the original).—From *Your Child's Self-Esteem*

"Helping our children grow up with strong self-esteem is the most important task of parenthood."—From *Self-Esteem*

"High self-esteem is the single most important ingredient for success in life."—From the educators' online *Journal of Extension*

And here are some tips in *Today I Am Lovable—365 Positive Activities for Kids,* by Diane Loomans. On January 4, the thought for the day is "I will notice everything that is unique about me today." On January 10, it's "Today I will ask for some tender, loving care." Apparently that's not enough, because the very next day's message is "I will let someone know one of my needs or wants today."

It's true that this little book reminds kids of worthy things like, "Friends are treasures." But the vast majority of the focus is like that of August 31: "Today I am willing to ask for what I want." It's an "all about me" world after all.

Building our child's self-esteem is the *most important* task of parenthood? *Nothing else* is as important? What about the idea of raising children who are compassionate and who esteem others? "Other-esteem" just doesn't seem to have much of a following in the parenting culture— or the culture in general. There certainly aren't any modern books about it that I can think of. I guess that's because we love to love ourselves.

And watch out, Mom and Dad: being careless about building self-esteem might not lead to your child being an ax murderer, but the parenting experts wouldn't have you take any chances.

Such is the mantra of the parenting culture. It manifests itself in countless ways, particularly in schools, which typically have self-esteem programs, assemblies, and curricula. These include "Esteem Builders," a popular self-esteem curriculum in which we are reminded—again— that high self-esteem is the single most important ingredient for success in life.

The self-esteem advocates may vary in pitch and intensity, but their message is the same: Children, no matter what they do, should always feel terrific about themselves as they are *right now*. (This also leads to one of the dictums of the parenting culture: "Criticize the child's behavior, never the child." The next chapter focuses on that one.)

Admittedly, some of these "experts" pay lip service to, for example, not overpraising a child. And in some quarters of American culture, the self-esteem movement is not only questioned, it's even satirized. Consider writer Al Franken's Stuart Smalley character on *Saturday Night*

Live. "I'm good enough, I'm smart enough, and, doggone it, people like me!" the affable, self-absorbed Smalley tells himself in the mirror each day.

But the self-esteem movement is hanging on tight in the parenting culture. This despite the fact that there is no evidence to show that it's the cure for all the ills it claims to be.

Just on the face of it, "super-kids who think they are super-terrific just as they are" pretty accurately describes the "in" group of seventh-grade girls who terrorize most junior highs. To paraphrase best-selling parenting author John Rosemond: no one wants to hang out with *anyone* who thinks he is absolutely terrific as is. So why are we training our kids to be those people?

Here's what one teacher wrote to me about what he sees every day—the results of the self-esteem movement:

> The common denominator is kids who are easily bored, self-centered to a frightening degree, and who have little respect for excellence or the effort required to achieve it. . . . They expect to be entertained at all times and to have the least bit of effort immediately validated. They respond to poor grades with anger or indifference and almost never say anything to indicate that they believe working longer or harder is the way to go.

We Love to Love Ourselves

This teacher's concern about the sour fruits of the self-esteem movement seems full of plain common sense. It shouldn't be too surprising that common sense is being backed up by research. In fact, it's becoming clear that too much self-esteem can create narcissistic, arrogant, even dangerous people.

In 2002, the *New York Times* reported that psychologists have found that D-level students often think pretty highly of themselves. And guess what? Serial rapists are just as likely to have high self-esteem as bank managers. The researchers quoted in that piece, Dr. Roy Baumeister of Case Western Reserve University and Dr. Brad Bushman of Iowa State University, have been doing research on self-esteem for years.

In 1998, they wrote in the *Journal of Personality and Social Psychology* that violent behavior, far from being minimized by high self-esteem, may be a result of, well, self-esteem on steroids. They found that it's those who think the most highly of themselves who may actually be the most dangerous.

In their study of more than five hundred college students, Baumeister and Bushman focused on narcissists, those who have a self-love that goes way beyond self-esteem. Interestingly, they argue that it's possible for the constant emphasis on self-esteem, particularly in the schools, to grow into excessive self-love, or narcissism. Dr. Bushman says, "If kids begin to develop unrealistically optimistic opinions of themselves and those beliefs are constantly rejected by others, their feelings of self-love could make these kids potentially dangerous to those around them." Narcissists are frightening. Baumeister and Bushman point out that people who are preoccupied with validating an excessively grand self-image apparently find criticism highly upsetting and lash out against the source of it.

Yet the parenting culture still holds that low self-esteem is responsible for violence, particularly among youth. So, for instance, in the wake of the Columbine killings we were treated to all sorts of speculation by experts that the teenage killers may have taken so many lives including their own because they had "low self-esteem." But, it appears that just the opposite was true. These young killers had the grandiose notion that they had the right to take the lives of others.

Dr. Nicholas Emler of the London School of Economics, a renowned expert on self-esteem, doesn't believe that self-esteem has to become narcissism before it becomes a problem. In his study titled *Self-Esteem: The Costs and Causes of Low Self-Worth,* he wrote that in fact, low self-esteem is actually *not* a risk factor for things like delinquency, violence (including child and partner abuse), drug use, alcoholism, and other pathologies.

While low self-esteem is a risk factor for suicide and depression, he found, it is only one among several related risk factors. But he did find that young people with high self-esteem are more likely to reject positive peer pressure, hold negative social views like racism, and to engage in risky behaviors like drunk driving. Emler writes, "Our language contains many unflattering words to describe people with high self-esteem, such as 'boastful,' 'arrogant,' 'smug,' 'self-satisfied,' and 'conceited'—terms that reflect a cultural accumulation of wisdom."

One big problem? High-self-esteem people tend to blame others for their failures. You see, since they are terrific, failure cannot be their fault.

One young reader wrote to me in response to a column I penned on self-esteem, "I'm thirteen, and 'self-esteem' is about the only word I hear out of teachers at my school." Another reader told me that, as a school counselor, he has to wage a daily battle against the dictates of the self-esteem mantra: "Trying to tell teachers anything about students assuming personal responsibility and earning respect is hopeless. They believe feelings are more important than hard work and wonder why their students don't know anything about math, even though their feelings about math are sky high." Such anecdotes aren't science, but when they pile up, one can't help but begin to notice that something is out of whack.

So why, in the parenting culture and in our education system, does there remain such a steadfast commitment to the benefits of self-esteem when the studies are not there to show its benefits, and there's so much evidence demonstrating problems? As the *New York Times* put it, "The accretion of evidence [against the self-esteem movement] has done little to dampen the enthusiasm of therapists, child-rearing experts and school administrators." As I said, it may just come down to the fact that we love to love ourselves.

And it may just be easier to praise a child than to teach him math.

There's something else. Dr. Jennifer Crocker of the University of Michigan has done excellent work on self-esteem. As she explained to me, there is clearly one benefit: people with high self-esteem do tend to be happier. Plainly, when you believe you are a terrific person *as is*, you probably will be more contented with your life. And it may be that in our culture today, personal happiness is considered such an important good, such a transcendent benefit, that it doesn't matter *what* we have to do, even to others, to achieve it for ourselves.

Is that the kind of happiness we want for our kids? Once again, try this: is "I'm happy because I'm absolutely terrific as I am" the kind of happiness we want our children's future spouses to have? Encouraging kids to feel terrific about themselves *just as they are* can have some pretty unappealing consequences. Many parents see that. Their question is, What now?

Esteeming for the Right Reasons

For starters, we do have to communicate to our kids that we love them unconditionally. Love is different from thinking our kids are terrific every moment. Love is action, and it's being committed to our kids and committed to doing good for them, no matter what happens. If our children think our love for them depends on their lovability, that could be pretty unnerving for them. They know there are days when they are not exactly "lovable." They have to know that even when they fail, even when they really mess up, we love them anyway. (And that's very different from how the world will respond to them when they mess up.)

Our love for them depends on our position as their parents, not on their worthiness, which means we love them even when they are *not* being terrific. In our house, when I ask my kids, "Why do I love you?" they reply, "Because God gave me to you." Right on.

Most important, we can teach our children that they have dignity and value because they are human beings who can and must make moral choices. They don't have value because they are "terrific every day and in every way," they have value precisely because they can choose to do better tomorrow.

The Crux of the Matter

When my daughter Victoria was preschool age, she seemed to be a real artist. She had manual dexterity and an eye for color that seemed far ahead of her years. I kept telling her—in order to build her self-confidence, I thought—"Honey, you are such a good artist." When she hit first grade, we were both, I think, ready to hear her art teacher tell her she was terrific. Instead, she got just a bit better than an average grade. She was devastated. What happened? Now I think I understand.

Carol Dweck is a renowned professor of psychology at Columbia University and the author of *Self-Theories: Their Role in Motivation, Personality and Development*. Her decades of research show that praising and valuing effort and striving to do better, rather than praising kids for being terrific as they are right now, are the keys to helping children do well in school and, by extension, in life. Here's an excerpt of an online interview she gave to *Education World* (*EW*) in 2000, which is, I think, worth quoting at length. Consider her insights in light of educators' and the parenting culture's consistently telling kids, "You are so smart!" or "You are such a good gymnast!" or "You are a terrific person!"

EW: Why is it that many students who succeed throughout their elementary school years suddenly seem to fall apart when they get to junior high or middle school?

Dweck: Many students look fine when things are easy and all is going well. But many students, even very bright ones, are not equipped to deal with challenges. When they hit more difficult work, as they often do when they get to junior high school or middle school, they begin to doubt their intelligence, they withdraw their effort, and their performance suffers. . . . They are scared that the difficulty they are experiencing means that they are in fact dumb. Furthermore, they are worried that if they try hard and still do poorly, they will really prove they're dumb.

The students who blossom at this time are the ones who believe that intellectual skills are things they can develop. They see the more difficult schoolwork as a challenge to be mastered through hard work, and they are determined to do what it takes to meet these new challenges.

Remember the claim that it's self-esteem that will determine the success or failure of every child. What does Dweck say to that?

Dweck: This is really fascinating. You might think that students who had a history of success would be the ones who loved challenges and had the ability to face them constructively.

But in fact, there is no relation between a history of success and seeking or coping with challenges. This is one of the great surprises in my research, and it goes to show that the ability to face challenges is not about your actual skills; it's about the mind-set you bring to a challenge.

We parents have to ask ourselves, Do we train our kids to see challenges as opportunities or something to be avoided because they are afraid of failing and losing the "smart" or "terrific" label?

And what about "Wow, you are smart!"? In Dweck's studies,

later grade school students worked on a task, succeeded nicely on the first set of problems, and received praise. Some received praise for their intelligence, and others received praise for their effort . . .

[But] when students were praised for their intelligence, they became so invested in looking smart that they became afraid of challenge. Most of them preferred a surefire success over a challenging opportunity to learn something important. When students were praised for their effort, 90 percent of them wanted the challenging learning opportunity.

When students then experienced a second, difficult set of problems, those who had been praised for their intelligence now told us they felt dumb. In other words, if the success meant they were smart, the failure meant to them that they were dumb. . . .

If self-esteem is that fragile, who needs it?

In contrast, the students who had been praised for their effort saw the setback not as a condemnation of their intellect, but as simply a signal for more effort. They realized that a harder task means harder work.

Dweck gave the students a third set of problems, and now the results were especially dramatic: those students who had been praised for their intelligence at the beginning did significantly worse, but those praised at the outset for *effort* did significantly better. The two groups, which had started out performing similarly, were now at dramatically different places.

Dweck is all for praising kids. She says we should just be wise about praising them for the right things. Further, and quite interesting to me as a mom of three girls, Dweck goes on to point out that all of this may have something to do with why girls tend to outperform boys in elementary school but tend to fall off by middle and certainly late high school. By college, men tend to do better, often significantly, than women. Dweck says that during the early, easier grades, typically more fidgety, less mature boys get messages that will help them later: "Sit still," "Pay attention," "Focus," and "Work harder." At the same time, more mature girls, so eager to please, get messages that don't help them in the face of a challenge: "You did such a good job!" "You are so smart!" Or, in an effort to build math and science skills in which girls seem to later flag, "You're so good at math!" or "You're so good at science!" It turns out that's a pretty bad idea.

Back to Victoria and her art. It seems she was scared of not impressing her art teacher the way she had impressed me. And it's possible that I simply overestimated her ability. In any event, she held back on her creativity, because she was afraid of making mistakes and having that "talented" label removed.

In a similar way, in his preschool years, Peter was a sponge for knowledge. He was an expert on the *Titanic* and other ill-fated ocean liners at age three. At age four, he searched out everything he could on skyscrapers, and at five it was space. So when he was six, we put him in a school for "gifted" students—and he hated every minute of it. He was aware of the label, of course. We thought his problem was that he didn't believe he was smart. The problem was that, without meaning to, we had taught him that we valued "smart" too much. He was afraid of losing that label and, therefore, our approval. (He was also afraid of doing algebra in first grade—and who wouldn't be?)

I have no doubt that there is a place for schools for gifted children. It just wasn't right for us. By the middle of second grade, he was out of that school and doing much better, particularly as I learned to encourage him to be challenged, not defeated, by his successes *and* his failures. Still, I'm sorry for that episode, because it has made it harder to rebuild his early love of learning. I guess I have to say that I failed, too, and I'm learning, but not defeated, by the experience.

I don't know if the high-school teacher who sent me this note was familiar with Carol Dweck's research, but she certainly echoes her conclusions:

> I keep telling my students, we all fail at various times in our lives. Successful people, with low or high self-esteem, are those individuals who have learned to accept defeat or failure as a learning experience. They do something constructive with the criticism or correction. I'd hate to think that my doctor might withhold bad news about my health for fear of making me feel bad about myself.

It's true that in the adult world, performance counts more than effort. No boss says, "Wow, you really tried hard on that annual report!" But the ability to face challenges, to see ourselves as capable of improving, is what often leads to better performance as well as more rewarding satisfaction in that performance.

Dr. Dweck's focus is on education. But surely we can extrapolate her results to suggest that conveying to our children that everything they do is terrific might actually give them a fragile self-esteem. It can rob them of the desire to improve and the ability to face challenges, including the challenge of becoming a better, more compassionate human being and, perhaps most important, a person who esteems others.

Esteeming, and Esteeming
Excellence in Others

I think one part of helping our kids to become such people—of pursuing our rescue mission for their hearts in this area—is helping them esteem excellence in others, whether in character or ability. This may keep our children striving to be better themselves, but it also teaches them to value what is objectively and truly good. They will be ennobled by contemplating the best, and their opportunity for joy will be expanded, because they will be able to find it in so many more places.

Further, learning to esteem excellence in others can provide at least some protection against two of the greatest soul destroyers out there—envy and jealousy.

I remember spending time with Victoria, looking at the artwork of other students who had competed in a schoolwide contest to have their drawings included in the school directory. (Victoria had not entered, despite my pleas.) We spent a great deal of time discussing and admiring the drawings by these other children, many of which were quite good. Victoria really seemed to appreciate the artistic sensibilities and skill of some of these other students. Though there are times when my kids can be little green monsters, this wasn't one of them. She admired the artwork and the students who did it, and it encouraged her that she herself could do better. She was determined to work hard to improve and be ready for the contest the next year.

Without criticizing our own children, there are countless positive ways we can help them esteem excellence in others.

By helping our children learn to esteem right and good and wholesome and encouraging things, whether about their world, or others, or finally themselves, we give them a gift. We pursue our rescue mission for their hearts. In contrast, when we teach them to esteem themselves "just as they are," we rob them of part of their development as human beings by inhibiting them from becoming better people tomorrow.

Centuries ago, Benjamin Franklin established what he called "The Thirteen Virtues." (That he himself apparently lacked some of them doesn't make them any less valid.) I think they are far more valuable than any emphasis on self-esteem.

They are:

Temperance. Eat not to dullness; drink not to elevation.

Silence. Speak not but what may benefit others or yourself; avoid trifling conversation.

Order. Let all your things have their places; let each part of your business have its time.

Resolution. Resolve to perform what you ought; perform without fail what you resolve.

Frugality. Make no expense but to do good to others or yourself; i.e., waste nothing.

Industry. Lose no time; be always employed in something useful; cut off all unnecessary actions.

Sincerity. Use no hurtful deceit; think innocently and justly, and, if you speak, speak accordingly.

Justice. Wrong none by doing injuries or omitting the benefits that are your duty.

Moderation. Avoid extremes; forbear resenting injuries so much as you think they deserve.

Cleanliness. Tolerate no uncleanness in body, clothes, or habitation.

Tranquility. Be not disturbed at trifles or at accidents common or unavoidable.

Chastity. Rarely use venery [sexual intercourse] but for health or offspring, never to dullness, weakness, or the injury of your own or another's peace or reputation.

Humility. Imitate Jesus and Socrates.

Personally, I don't agree with the "rarely use venery" clause for those who are married, but in all else, this a fine list of "other-esteem" traits. How different, and how much better, than today's cult of self-esteem.

For those who desire their own happiness and pleasure above all else, and who want to raise children who feel the same way, the self-esteem movement is a panacea. For those who want their children to esteem and be responsible toward others, to find real joy in life, to avoid the soul-stunting practice of self-worship, it's time to break free from the parenting culture's devotion to the cult of self-esteem.

Parenting Check

We need to think about how we praise our kids. What kind of language do we use? Is our praise going to help them face challenges, or might it make them more susceptible to life's curveballs?

We might ask ourselves, or we might even ask our children, why do they have value? The answers we get from our kids may not be very articulate, but we might at least get a sense of whether they think they matter because of something they do well, or if they have an inkling, at least, of their intrinsic worth as human beings. Maybe they've never even thought about that question, but it's a good one.

Then consider asking them why they think you love them. Do they think your love for them depends on what they do or achieve or simply on your unchangeable position as their parent?

7

Misbehavior and Other Matters of the Heart

Do you know why children misbehave? The folks at the Aware Parenting Institute (awareparenting.com), an online resource for child-centered parenting, do. "We can explain almost all unacceptable behavior in children by one of the following three factors: The child is attempting to fill a legitimate need, the child lacks information, or the child is suffering from stress or unhealed traumas."

Not to be outdone, the parenting experts at Kansas State University have found twice as many reasons why kids misbehave. Their Wonder-Wise Parent website (ksu.edu/wwparent/wondhome.htm) says kids behave badly because "they have been rewarded for their misbehavior, they have copied what their parents do, they are testing whether their parents will enforce the rules, they are asserting themselves and their independence, they are protecting themselves . . . or they feel bad about themselves."

Oops—wait! The experts at the University of Minnesota have found seven reasons why children misbehave (extension.umn.edu): they learn by observing others, they're growing up, they feel threatened, they feel bad about themselves, they are tired, or hungry, or sick.

Now let's fast forward from child to adult. You're at work, and your boss is yelling at you, making ridiculous demands and otherwise making your life miserable. Will you go home to your spouse and say, "Wow, I really feel bad for my boss. He must be trying to fill some legitimate need." Or maybe you'll say, "Gee, he must feel really bad about himself!"

No, you're going to say, "My boss is a selfish jerk! I'm sorry if he's upset about something, but he still has no right to act that way."

And you would be right.

Fortunately, we treat our children much differently than we treat our bosses. (Or at least we should, although too many parents seem to forget their children are not their bosses.) For one thing, we love our kids. For another, it's our job to train them so that *they* don't grow up to be people who selfishly terrorize others.

Civilizing Children

In other words, it's our job as parents to civilize our children.

How do we do that? For starters, we dare not consistently make excuses for them, or to them, for their bad behavior. Yes, sometimes they misbehave because they are tired. Other times, their behavior might be due to immaturity (in which case, it shouldn't be called bad behavior). But many times, children behave badly for the very same reasons adults do: because they can be selfish and self-absorbed, because they want their way and they want it *now*. Once again, I'm reminded of young Veruca in *Willy Wonka & the Chocolate Factory*, who says, "But I want it *now*, Daddy!" And terrified Daddy always complies.

The parenting culture seems loath to recognize that the human condition is one of selfishness, that it hasn't changed much since the beginning of time, and that this applies to our kids, too. This used to be called original sin. Here's how we know it's real: no one I know has ever heard anyone say about another, "Boy he's having a bad day—everything has gone wrong for him. That must be why he's being particularly kind and generous." Or, "My that little girl must be worn out with exhaustion. No wonder she's being such a cheerful little angel." That's ridiculous—precisely because it's our true self that comes out when there are no inhibitions holding it in. And it's often not very pretty.

Still not convinced? Have you ever heard a child argue "It's not fair!" because he's actually interested in matters of justice? The reason a two-year-old stomping his foot and demanding his way can be at least a little amusing is because he's only three feet tall and thirty pounds. Translate that into six feet tall and two hundred pounds, and you've got a problem.

Of course, kids lack knowledge and are immature. If we adults give our knee a good thwack against a table, we might limp for a minute and say, "It's okay, it's okay," whereas a child might scream bloody murder. That's not misbehavior, it's immaturity.

And, yes, sometimes they are just exhausted. I have a daughter who sometimes hits "the tipping point" if she gets overtired. She just dissolves into tears, and the only thing to do is put her to bed and remind myself for the hundredth time that she needs more rest than the others.

Sometimes, it's just fun for kids to push that envelope. When Victoria was about three, we were organizing closets. I gave her some clothes and instructed her to go put them away in her own room. She dutifully left with the clothes only to come back several minutes later with a solemn look on her face. "Did you put your clothes away, dear?" I asked. "No, Mom," she replied. "God told me I didn't have to." Now that was a gutsy way of trying to get out of work. She thought she'd dropped the nuclear bomb of excuses.

Wrong.

And sometimes they model what they see. I walked into my office one day, where my children also have their computer, and found Olivia, then about two, on the kids' PC. Obviously frustrated that she hadn't yet figured out how to make the thing work, she was banging the keyboard, saying, "Stupid, stupid, stupid!" That is not bad behavior. It just means Mom has to be a bit more careful about her own reaction to "computer events."

So, yes, there are lots of reasons children misbehave. But while all that's true, we have to also recognize that many times our children behave badly because their characters are flawed, just like ours. And it's our job as parents to help them recognize and guard against those flaws.

"Criticize the Behavior, Not the Child"

This leads us to one off the most tenaciously held pieces of accepted wisdom in today's parenting culture: Criticize the behavior, not the child. The website justforkidsonly.com tells parents, "Do not criticize your child. If at all, criticize your child's behavior." Psychologist David Goodman of Oak Park, Illinois, echoes the sentiment when he writes, "Don't criticize your child . . . only the behavior is bad" (familyshrink .com). The same message is preached at the Art of Positive Parenting website (positiveparenting.com): "Separate the child from his behavior" and "Don't blame or shame."

I hate to criticize, but these folks don't make sense.

Pediatrician Donna D'Alessandra tells parents through the Virtual Hospital website (vh.org) not to criticize their children because "criticism can make a child feel bad." Well, no doubt. This used to be called developing a conscience. But we modern parents are so desperate for our kids to feel good about themselves *all the time*, no matter what they do or don't do, that we are loath to let them feel bad about themselves, even when they *should* feel bad about themselves. What a terrible disservice to them.

Developing a conscience can be a painful thing. But helping our children do so is imperative to our rescue mission in their lives. It is, after all, that bad feeling—or conscience—that over time helps a child stop the particular bad behavior, not just because of the possible pain of punishment, but also because it causes pain to his heart. Yes, the process may hurt, but it shapes the child's character and very humanity.

Sure, there can be extenuating circumstances, but it's safe to say that a normal, healthy child's behavior comes from the heart. Where else could it originate? If we see an eight-year-old stand up to bullies who are teasing his friend, we rightly see that as virtuous, indicating good things about the disposition of that child's heart. (In fact, it's knowing how much more difficult that was for him than walking away that makes his virtue clear.) We don't separate *that* behavior from the child. Likewise, if a seven-year-old is deliberately nasty to her little sister, doesn't that behavior also come from the child's heart? I mean, it didn't get dropped off by Federal Express.

It's true, a child may have seen bad behavior modeled anywhere—on television, by peers, even parents. But the reason a child copies it so naturally when he doesn't copy loving or virtuous behavior as effortlessly is because unkind behavior comes so easily to us, like second nature—or perhaps first nature. To pretend otherwise or to sugarcoat it and call it something other than bad behavior does nothing to help a child.

A child may learn, "I shouldn't feel bad about myself," even when she's behaved badly. A child may have her bad behavior routinely labeled as something else. Or a child may come to believe that she and her behavior are separate, so she's not responsible for it. That is a child who may have her conscience deadened over time. And a deadened conscience is poison to the heart. No wonder there is a growing body of evidence that children raised in the "I feel good about myself" world of self-esteem are more likely to become narcissistic, arrogant adults.

Do you want your daughter to marry someone who believes his behavior comes from his heart, or one who thinks that he and his behavior are somehow two separate things?

Interpreting Matters of the Heart

If we are to persevere in our rescue mission for our children's hearts, we must ensure that our children are alive to—even on the lookout for—the shortcomings of their hearts.

The flip side of that, of course, is encouraging the good things we see in their hearts. All the more so because those good things come less naturally. "You are being really generous to your sister. Terrific!" "You're being patient on these long errands—I appreciate it." "I know it was difficult to be kind to your classmate when he's been unkind to you, but doesn't that make you feel better than being mean?"

We might, for instance, help them see that they are particularly sensitive or tenderhearted, and point out that while that can be a great blessing, it might also make them think others are being critical when they really are not. Or we might help our kids understand that they have a gift for compassion and help them find ways to express or magnify that gift.

At other times, I might point out to my kids that they have something unattractive in their hearts. I might say, "Dear, you are being really unkind to your brother." To another, I might say, "You are being spiteful right now. Please think about what is going on in that heart of yours."

But how can we do any of these things if we separate the behavior from the child? Sometimes—stand back, everyone—I actually let my kids know they should be ashamed of themselves. In other words (sorry,

Dr. D'Alessandra), there are times when I want them to feel bad about themselves.

I might help my kids see that they struggle with jealousy or unkindness toward a sibling by saying, "Honey, the next time you find yourself fussing at your sister, think about what is in your heart at that moment. If I could look into it right then, would I see something of beauty? Or would I see something that wasn't attractive at all?"

I sometimes help them see that problem areas can be transformed into something good. Willfulness can be become determination, for example, or impatience can be transformed into a healthy drive for excellence. But we cannot do these things if we separate the behavior from the child.

I think some of the "Criticize the behavior, not the child" dictates come from a fear of *defining* a child by her behavior. That's a legitimate concern. I would not, for example, tell my kids that they were mean or selfish people. In every moment, they have the ability to do better, to be better, and I let them know that and encourage them to those ends.

I simply try to help them understand the tendency of their hearts when an appropriate opportunity presents itself. This does not mean I spend every minute analyzing what's going on in there. That could take all day. Sometimes they have to just be told, "Knock it off right now!" But I do pick times to talk to them about their hearts, and during those times, I make sure my kids know they are loved unconditionally, not because they are good or when they are good, but simply because they are my children.

Full disclosure (again): only a few months ago, one of my children was displaying a terrible attitude. I said, "Honey, what's going on in that heart of yours right now?" The answer? "I hate that 'heart' talk, Mom—we all do! Who cares what's going on in my dumb heart, anyway?" Well, I care even if she doesn't. And just because it's annoying doesn't mean it's not effective! The fact that it's annoying may actually be a sign of its effectiveness. How important the heart issue is if we are to be successful in our rescue mission for our kids.

The parenting culture says otherwise. In *What to Expect: The Toddler Years,* part of the wildly best-selling What to Expect series, the authors say rightly that children "need to feel that parental love won't be diminished or withdrawn if kids misbehave," which, they argue, is why the behavior but not the child should be criticized. Yet it seems to me that following this advice can lead to a child's feeling accepted *only* for good behavior. A child may very well have some sense that he is being wholly selfish, or mean, or jealous at any one moment. So what if Mom and Dad—who tell him he's always a nice person deep down whatever his behavior—find out he's not *always* such a nice person after all? That could be quite a scary thought for a little one.

Maybe it's better to let our kids know that their behavior comes from the heart, and that when sometimes they are *not* being nice people at all at the moment, that's not okay—and we love them anyway.

What a gift it is to help our children see both the strengths and the frailties of their own hearts and know we love them so much. If they believe that their behavior is separate from their hearts, we can't give them that gift. And that means we limit our ability to pursue our rescue mission in their lives.

It's also helpful for our kids to know that we continue this self-examination in our own lives. For one thing, we want to model good behavior. And when we blow it—even if it never gets as bad as my tantrum at the pumpkin patch—we need to be able to apologize to our kids and let them know that we're works in progress, too. But we also need to let them know that our failures don't give them the right to stop striving to do better.

So, sometimes at night as we pray together, I'll ask God to give my children patience with me, to help them understand that I, like them, am a sinner in need of a savior. I pray that my sin will not be a stumbling block for them. Now, I don't pray this with them every single night—I don't want them to think I'm a complete idiot. But I want them to know that I struggle with frailties of the heart, too.

A "Disorder" to Explain the Disorder of the Heart

In a strange way, the parenting culture has attempted to fill an obvious breach when it comes to behavior problems. Since the experts refuse to attribute bad behavior to a child's heart, and instead seem to believe that a child is capable of being a perfect little dear if only he is exposed to the right "techniques," that leaves them with a contradiction: they have to come up with some explanation for behavior problems. I mean, if such problems don't come from a flawed heart—children don't have flawed hearts, after all—and if every possible modern parenting technique has been tried, what's going on? What if, after being reasoned with, having their self-esteem built, being given lots of choices, maybe even being put in time-out, the kids are still screaming, refusing to share toys, disobeying their parents, or far worse? The only possibility left is . . . a disorder!

Thus, we have today's most common children's psychiatric condition, according to the website of pediatric psychiatrist Dr. James Chandler of the Royal College of Physicians and Surgeons of Canada (klis.com/chandler). Oppositional defiant disorder (ODD) is the label attached to 5 percent of American children, and that number is rising fast. A case study is Marianne:

Marianne is now four years old . . .
Marianne begins her day by getting up early and making noise. Her father unfortunately has mentioned how much this bothers him. So

she turns on the TV or, if that has been mysteriously disconnected, bangs things around until her parents come out. [At breakfast] Marianne does not like what is being served once it is placed in front of her. When [her parents] are very rushed, she is more stubborn and might refuse [breakfast] altogether. It would be a safe bet that she would tell her mom that the toast tastes like poop. This gets her the first time-out of the day.

In the mornings, she goes to preschool or goes off with her grandmother or over to her aunt's. Otherwise Marianne's mother is unable to do anything. [Marianne] gets along with other children as long as she can tell them what to do.

Most of the afternoon with Marianne is spent chasing her around trying to wear her out. It doesn't seem to work, but it is worth a try. . . . Marianne loves the bedtime battle. She also loves to go to the mall. But she never gets to go there, or hardly anywhere else either. She acts up so badly that her family is very embarrassed. . . . It is hard to know who is more excited about Marianne going to school next year, her mother or Marianne!

I am not a clinician, I don't even play one on TV, but I think it's at least a good bet that Marianne does not have a disorder at all. Or rather, she has a disorder, but it's a disorder of the heart, and her parents will not help her with her predicament. What is clear from an extensive description of Marianne is that her parents are in no way attempting to exert any authority in their child's life. The mother may invoke a time-out, which doesn't seem to bother Marianne in the least, but in the end she *always* gives in to Marianne.

It seems very possible that little Marianne is an incredibly willful, even difficult, child who has learned to control those around her and who displays the thoroughly human tendency of loving every minute of it—though the odds are she's a miserable child. We *know* her parents are miserable. (Just imagine living with such a tyrant.)

I don't understand why Marianne's parents utterly cower in the face of their four-year-old. Why not attempt to exert responsibility and save their four-year-old from herself, before handing her over to a diagnosis of oppositional defiant disorder? Perhaps because they've bought into the paradigm of the parenting culture, and they're separating the behavior from the child.

Here is the clinical description of ODD:

A pattern of negativistic, hostile, and defiant behavior lasting at least six months, during which four or more of the following are present:

1. Often loses temper.
2. Often argues with adults.
3. Often actively defies or refuses to comply with adults' requests or rules.
4. Often deliberately annoys people.
5. Often blames others for his or her mistakes or misbehavior.
6. Is often touchy or easily annoyed by others.
7. Is often angry and resentful.
8. Is often spiteful or vindictive.

Well, I would argue, as I did in chapter 1, that our entire paradigm on child behavior is shifting, so that what was once unacceptable is acceptable and what was once really unacceptable is now a disorder.

Keep in mind that while there is more to the diagnostic criteria than just these points, only four of these behaviors need be present to start a child down the path of ODD. ODD could describe a whole lot of kids. When I wrote a column on this topic, one mom wrote to tell about what was once her extraordinarily disruptive little one. This child pushed me to the point of taking her to child psychiatrist when she was about two and half. To this day, I am grateful for a doctor who recognized a normal, healthy, stubborn, and strong-willed child. It was I that needed the lessons in rearing a child with these qualities, lessons that I still use on her. And today, she is a nineteen-year-old beauty, with wonderful manners (and more self-confidence than is healthy, I think sometimes), who returned this spring from ten months serving on the crew of a medical humanitarian aid ship in West Africa and leaves in about thirty days for her freshman year of college.

Today that little girl might very well have been diagnosed with ODD.

The Confidence to Pursue Our Children's Hearts

I do believe that children can have very real pathologies that can interfere, sometimes drastically, with behavior. I'm even convinced that psychological conditions go undiagnosed in some children. I also believe that, in certain instances, medication or other therapy can be appropriate, even life saving (although I think extraordinary care must be taken here, as we know far less about how psychotropic drugs affect kids than adults).

But I'm concerned that, as Jeffrey Kluger wrote in *Time* magazine,

Just a few years ago, psychologists couldn't say with certainty that kids were even capable of suffering from depression the same way adults do. Now, according to PhRMA, a pharmaceutical trade group, up to 10 percent of all American kids may suffer from some mental illness. . . . Other children are receiving diagnoses and medication for obsessive-compulsive disorder, social-anxiety disorder, post-traumatic stress disorder, pathological impulsiveness, sleeplessness, phobias and more.

So, how to sort this out? One of the best books I've read on these issues is *Blame It on the Brain: Distinguishing Chemical Imbalances, Brain Disorders, and Disobedience* by Edward T. Welch. The main thrust of Welch's book is that some disorders, like attention deficit disorder (ADD), can be real. After exhausting other possibilities (including behavioral, moral, and spiritual problems), the issues at hand may be attributed to a disorder of the brain, which sometimes—*sometimes*—can be helped with medication or other treatment. But he cautions against parents seeking treatment so they won't have to deal with the child's problems, instead of (rightly) seeing it as a way of getting the child to the point where parental interventions will have an effect.

Parents don't have to be captives of factions in the culture that declare "you must medicate" or "you must not medicate" your kids. They do have to take responsibility for making the most informed decision they can when it comes to their own children. And if they decide their child has a medical problem that needs treatment, their goal must always be to bring their child to a point where they can reach the child's heart, not to a point where medication can do their job for them. Because it can't.

In any event, just because some children have real organic problems that keep them from functioning normally is no justification for the fact that today, behavioral and school-related problems are most often seen as physical disorders of the body or brain and almost never as disorders of the human heart.

This view has had an inevitable byproduct: parents who can't accept that their child, who may have no behavioral problems, is just a little different. The minute a teacher says, "Gee, he doesn't seem to join in play with the other kids very easily," Mom and Dad panic and run to psychotherapists. It seems that almost any child who deviates even slightly from the norm gets a label and renewed attempts to make him "better, faster, stronger." But sometimes children just need help to flourish on their own terms.

Wendy Mogel talks about this in *The Blessing of a Skinned Knee*. She writes:

> Parents feel hope if their restless child is actually hyperactive, their dreamy child has ADD, their poor math student has a learning disorder, their shy child has a social phobia, their wrongdoing son has "intermittent explosive disorder." If there is a diagnosis, specialists and tutors can be hired, drugs given, treatment plans made, and parents can maintain an illusion that the imperfection can be overcome. Their faith in their child's unlimited potential is restored.

This, I think, is the tragedy: minor behavioral problems are attributed to tiredness, hunger, or frustration, but not to the heart. Major behavioral problems are attributed to a malfunction in the brain, but not to the heart. The experts tenaciously hang on to the notion that the right techniques, or the right medication, or the right excuses, can yield a better child. That view is, after all, precisely why we need the experts to tell us what those right things are—right?

The parenting culture is loath to understand that many behavior problems come from the heart. And that is a tragedy to the extent it keeps parents from better reaching the hearts of their children.

Parenting Check

As a parent, I find myself seeing virtue in my children when they act well, but often wanting to come up with excuses for them when they act badly, even when there isn't an excuse. We all do that. Hey, we love our kids, and while we don't want that love to be blind, it's probably not a bad idea if it's a little nearsighted from time to time.

The question is, are we always looking for excuses for our child's bad behavior? Does it scare us to think there might not be some reason for the behavior that we can't easily "fix"? Does it bother us to think behavior might come from a flawed heart, or does that understanding encourage us in our rescue mission for our child's heart?

8

When Did "No" Become a Dirty Word?

One morning when Olivia was about two, I was sitting down to work on my book when she asked for a piece of cheese. I said no. I didn't offer her an alternative snack. I didn't give her choices. I didn't try to distract her instead of saying no. Nor did I justify my action with an explanation she couldn't possibly understand about how close it was to lunchtime. I mean, even if she could comprehend that lunch was coming, it's not as if she'd say, "Oh, now I get your point, and I agree with you, Mom. Thanks for clearing that up!"

I just said, "No, dear, no cheese." That was it. She complied and, amazingly, she seemed to survive the incident with her psyche intact. I say "amazingly" because, according to the parenting culture, I did everything wrong. By just saying no, I committed a big no-no. If we accept that we are on a rescue mission for our kids, we have to change that thinking.

Here's what the parenting culture tells us about "no":

"Limit your 'no's' to situations that threaten the well-being of your toddler, of another person, or of your home . . . with each 'no,' always offer a 'yes' in the form of an alternative."—From *What to Expect: The Toddler Years*

Betsy of South Orange, New Jersey, was praised by *Parenting* magazine because she "could stop almost any unruly behavior by excitedly showing her [toddler] son . . . a 'wow-whee!' item" instead of saying no.—From parenting.com.

In his article titled "Seven Ways to Avoid Saying 'No' to Your Children," author and educator James Sutton tells us to "empower them [the kids] with choices, redirect them, and sometimes let them make plans for the whole family, say for a weekend outing, and let them know that parents aren't perfect."—docspeak.com

As if kids needed reminding of that latter point.

Parents need to find "positive, creative alternatives to saying 'no' when setting limits." Use "the look" or the "I mean business" voice instead of no. But don't use those things too often either—they can damage the child's self-esteem. Remember, "the fewer the 'no's' the better your day goes."—Parenting guru Dr. William Sears to a La Leche League conference in Chicago

In his book *Discipline,* Dr. Sears refers to no as the "n-word." So has no really become something that can't be mentioned in polite company?

Even some of these experts say that some nos are necessary for kids. But in those rare cases, they argue, it's best to disguise the nos whenever possible. Yes, according to the experts, no is a no-no.

I'm hardly arguing that no is a cure-all or some sort of magic word. No parent in his right mind, for instance, would rely on no to protect a two-year-old from Drano. I, for one, have more than a few latches on drawers, and the cleaning solutions are on high shelves. Nor am I suggesting that we look for ways to say no just for the heck of it. That's not rocket science.

But neither is the strange idea that a toddler should be told no *only* when the well-being of persons or property is at stake. For starters, there may be plenty of times when a child needs to be told no, simply because someone else's needs are rightly being put before his, or his needs, which he cannot understand, are being met when his wants are not.

Question: Has our culture come to reject these notions for both children and adults?

Answer: In our culture, we want to please ourselves, and so, it seems, we will do anything to please our children, too.

For the Joy of the "Experience"?

I've fallen right into that trap. One recent Christmas, I invited Victoria and Madeleine to come with me to pick out Christmas ornaments as a wedding present for a young couple. Because it was a special wedding gift, we went to a special store—Neiman Marcus. I quickly made my ornament choices, but my girls said, "Mom, can we each pick out an ornament?" Here's what went through my head: It's Christmastime. Wouldn't it be nice for them to each pick out an ornament, maybe if it's not too expensive? "Okay, girls," I agreed.

Off they trotted, wanting to buy every ornament they saw. They had no idea what to look for. At least they decided to choose ornaments that couldn't break, which was some small victory. Still, they ended up with unattractive ornaments I could not believe they really wanted. That left me suddenly in the position of paying thirty dollars for a couple of ornaments we didn't need and I didn't care for. Why? Because I didn't want to say no to my kids.

For me, this wasn't about a material possession. I say no all the time to material things, with little squeamishness. In this case, it was the experience. I'm big on experiences, and I want my kids to have all kinds of precious, meaningful ones, particularly Christmas experiences. That's what I was saying yes to—the experience of picking out some unwanted, overpriced Christmas ornament at a fancy store, simply because we were there.

Had I not offered to take them with me on that shopping trip, they wouldn't have thought twice about it. Had they been dreaming for days about picking out a special ornament? No. They just happened to be there, they saw shiny pretty things, they asked for one (why not?), and I said yes. Slam dunk.

I had really blown it. I considered returning the ornaments and making some ourselves instead, but my craft prowess is limited. Besides, I was responsible for what had happened, not the girls. I'd told them they could pick out ornaments, and I couldn't go back on my word.

On the way home, I realized I was out thirty bucks and up a few ornaments that I would never have chosen myself and that my girls could easily have done without. I also realized that I was completely furious with myself, all because I didn't want to say no to a "precious moment" my kids didn't even care about. And my girls had learned, "Hey, we're in an overpriced store. Let's get stuff." I learned an expensive lesson. Or maybe a cheap one.

So, it's not that I am particularly confident (or particularly hardhearted!) about saying no. I'm just learning, I hope, to be more comfortable saying no when it's necessary. I have to continually remind myself about the difference between what the parenting culture says I should do and what I know is right in my heart. Often I quite literally think through the long-term and very different consequences of both approaches. I frequently ask myself, "Which route is going to advance my rescue mission for my child's heart?" That helps a lot, as does remembering that Neiman Marcus bill.

Anyway, back to the two-year-old who wanted cheese. One winter night, Olivia wanted her jammies on and brought me half a pair of summer pajamas, in which she would freeze. I pulled out the appropriate pajamas and, over her howls of protest, put them on her. (Unfortunately for her, I wasn't worried about passing up a precious moment in that instance.) I dressed her, ignoring her caterwauling, and deposited her in her crib. Seventeen seconds after that, when I started reading to her and her then four-year-old sister, she forgot all about the incident. A few minutes later, she was cozily and warmly asleep for the night.

Positive Parenting?

Is that how most parents would have handled it? I'm not sure, but I do know what the parenting culture teaches. Here's what Karen Sims at the *Positive Parenting* newsletter had to say about a similar situation, with the admonishment to always seek to "empower" the child:

> Give choices, not orders. A father, trying to change an eighteen-month-old's diaper against the wishes of the child, offered the child a choice of which room to have the change made. The child chose a room, but once in the room, balked again at the diaper change. The father continued with his plan to empower the child and asked, "Which bed?" The child pointed to a bed, the diaper was changed, and the ongoing power struggle about diaper changes was ended.

That power struggle was ended, all right. The eighteen-month-old won. For one thing, that's got to be kind of scary for a toddler. Moreover, what could have, and should have, been a quick and simple diaper change became a household tour.

The incident seems minor, but is the father going to walk the house every time the kid needs a clean diaper? Once the child figures out he's in control of his dad, those walks will only get longer. Both the dad and the child learned something in that exchange: the father couldn't do something as basic as changing a diaper without the tiny child's approval. I don't understand why not.

I've heard parents say that they just want peace with their preschoolers or toddlers. They'll start enforcing rules, they say, "when he's a bit older." That transition, even if possible, is going to be exhausting and miserable for both parent and child. In the meantime, I'm guessing it's pretty hard to keep peace with a toddler when you're consistently giving in to her.

The big thing these parents don't realize is that by not doing anything, they are very much doing something. Daily, they train the child, *and themselves*, to give the child his way to keep the peace. That training will create some destructive and almost impossible to break habits.

This is no way to conduct a rescue mission.

There are, it seems to me, a couple of reasons why such thinking is so common. First, we as parents are utterly—and dangerously—unconvinced that we really do know better than our kids, that we really have authority in their lives. We looked at that truth in chapter 3, "I'm on Your Side."

The second reason is that we in the United States are committed to the cult of the always contented child. As Dr. Shaw writes in *The Epidemic*, we are simply terrified that our children might experience irritation, frustration, anger, disappointment, sadness, or any other negative emotion, even if having and learning to handle these emotions are part of the journey of being human.

We are devoted to the idea that life is about our pleasure. Shouldn't that then be true for our kids, too? Whether it's our physical appetites for sex or food, our material appetites for acquisitions, our appetites to vent and act upon our emotions at will or demand that our desires be met—somehow we think that "no" is unnatural.

Instead of seeing "no" as protecting body and soul, we see it as crushing the human spirit. And what's good for us is good for our kids. Of course, it's not really good for us *or* our kids.

Put another way, the idea that nos must always be delivered dripping in sugar—besides being an utterly exhausting proposition—comes from the unfortunate notion that telling our children no is a bad thing in and of itself. We've come to believe that no may be a necessary evil, but it is an evil to be avoided as much as possible.

Adversity Is a No-No, Too

Timothy Stuart and Cheryl Bostrom, award-winning educators and authors of the thoughtful book *Children at Promise: 9 Principles to Help Kids Thrive in an At-Risk World,* carefully studied successful adults, which they defined as people who contribute positively to the moral and social fabric of society. The authors looked at their backgrounds. They found that adversity was consistently part of the "success story." Over and over again they found that adversity had produced richness in the characters of the people they studied, as long as they had loving adult relationships to help interpret that adversity.

Today's parents are typically terrific at the "loving adult relationships" part of that equation. But we will do anything to protect our kids from the slightest disappointment, let alone true adversity. In the process, it seems, we may be stunting our children's humanity. No one goes looking for adversity for their kids. But what these authors say is that when it does inevitably come, our job is not to be terrified of it but to help our children think rightly about it.

That does not seem to be the view of the thirteen faculty members at Tufts University who wrote *Proactive Parenting*. I couldn't find anything about saying no anywhere in the book. Instead, the authors say, "To ensure follow-through, use 'directives' sparingly. We suggest that parents try rephrasing directives to emphasize the need rather than the imperative: 'You need to sit down now' may garner cooperation, whereas 'sit down!' invites challenge." It does? And is inviting a challenge from a young child always to be avoided? I guess, according to these folks, the answer is yes.

Here's how they suggest handling a young child and a puddle. Remember, according to the parenting culture, a mom or dad can't say no and risk challenging or crossing her will. Instead, they must have an always contented child, and so they must not allow adversity or disappointment into her life, even regarding something as simple as a puddle.

> Consider again the example of taking a walk with your child and coming upon a puddle. What if she's dressed in good shoes and gears up for a fight when you tell her she can't jump in? What are you going to do? Threaten her? Grab her? Drag her away? Attempts to control an excited child may turn into a contest of wills. Here may be a perfect time to guide her by redirecting her attention: "What could you do with the puddle besides jump in it?" "Here's a stone; what can you do with that?" "How about a stick?"

Who are these parents whose only options are threatening, grabbing, or dragging? They are parents of children who have never heard the word "no" without having it disguised beyond recognition, much less learned to respect a parent's clear and firm "directive." These are children who are well aware that their parents do not want to cross their wills.

I'm happy to say that I know moms and dads who would simply say, "No, dear, no going into the puddle," and whose children would—gasp—neither go into the puddle nor throw a fit about it. It concerns me that the folks who wrote *Proactive Parenting* apparently have not met such parents and kids.

What if that puddle is in the middle of a parking lot with cars whizzing by? For that matter, I for one do not have the time or unlimited energy it would take to stop at each and every puddle and go through this exercise with a three-year-old.

The bottom line is that the Tufts University faculty members who collaborated on the book are suggesting that parents go to the extremes of what I call the "puddle exercise" with a three-year-old to avoid, at all costs, saying "No, you just can't" to a preschooler.

Houston, we have a problem. Again.

We are, after all, talking about a child and a puddle. What happens when we're talking about a teenager and a car?

I have a friend who told me that her husband will not put their eighteen-month-old child in the stroller when she doesn't want to be put there, because the child will fuss. Mom does it instead, the child fusses, the family survives. That may also be a symptom of the larger problem: parents who have lost the notion that legitimately saying no is a *beneficial* part of good parenting, not just a necessary evil.

Parents often compartmentalize. There are things we love to do with our kids: quiet midnight talks when they have trouble sleeping, taking them to the circus, making cookies together, family vacations, or movies at home on Friday nights. We see these as the bonus to parenting, the icing on the cake.

Then there are the things we tolerate, activities that are not as fulfilling but are necessary for taking care of business. These are the things we have to do, like getting them up and onto the school bus on time, helping with math homework, and getting them to their various after-school activities.

Finally, there are the things we *hate* to do, but do because we have to. It's the dark side of parenting, the ugly stuff we pull out of the closet only when we have to, and then put back in as fast as we can. It's saying no. "You can't have it, you can't do it, you're not going, you can't act that way, you may not play before piano practice or homework." Just no. It gives us the shivers. But it shouldn't.

Parents are finally realizing—or maybe just remembering—that too much materialism is downright bad for kids. This isn't just about the teenager in Beverly Hills who gets a BMW when he turns sixteen, or the seventh grader in New York City who takes her friends on a shopping spree at Saks for her birthday. Those parents are beyond the pale.

Even middle-class youngsters, we're realizing, are getting too darn much stuff. Toys, electronic gadgets, cell phones—it's over the top. Many parents who can afford to give their kids these things, are, it seems, beginning to see that such largesse creates selfishness, a sense of life being handed to a child on a silver platter, a presumption that a child is owed such things. Lately, parenting books and magazines are full of admonitions against giving too many material goods to children of all ages. We're beginning to hear, even from the parenting culture, that denying a child material goods he doesn't need can have incredibly positive therapeutic benefits.

That's terrific. But it doesn't go far enough. Being legitimately told "No, it's not your turn," "No, you can't stay ten more minutes," "No, you can't act like that" can have great benefits, too. It teaches a child self-discipline and delayed gratification, and lets her know that there are times when the needs and rights of others legitimately trump her desires of the moment.

This doesn't mean we can't give our kids a ten-minute warning. We don't have to drop nos like atom bombs. The goal is not to make them hurt. The goal is to not be afraid of no.

Sure, we parents love to give good things to our kids. It's fun to see their faces light up as they gobble down ice cream, ride a roller coaster, or get to stay up an hour later than usual to watch a favorite movie. I am simply making the case that wise parents view legitimate nos as a good thing, too.

Allowing children, even young children, to experience adversity or discontent or to have their wills crossed not only creates more peace and less exhaustion for parent and child, but also allows children to grow in the richness of what it means to be a human being, and prepares them just a bit for the road ahead of them. Refusing to let a little one have his way in all things, even in such simple things as forgoing a puddle, getting a diaper changed, or being placed in a stroller, not only gets the family moving more easily, but trains the child and the parents how to respond appropriately to each other, and trains the child to live in a world of rules (the vast majority of which are made up by someone other than himself). And many of which come down to: *no.*

Consider two children: one learns early on to respect "no" because she sees that her parents value it and she learns over time to value it herself. She believes it to be a good thing, protective of body and soul, even though it's not always pleasant. Another child has rarely heard "no" and then only when it's disguised or sugarcoated so much it's barely recognizable. This child may grow to believe that "no" is somehow unfair, a violation of his rights.

Which child will find more joy in life? Which one do you want your child to marry?

Stubborn, Irritable, Argumentative . . .

In 2000, Chris Knoester, then a doctoral student at Penn State, did an analysis of an ongoing long-term study of married couples, looking at behavior problems in their children. (The study was begun by Dr. Alan Booth and Dr. Paul Amato in 1980.)

Knoester found that kids who were routinely prone to temper tantrums or were often stubborn, irritable, argumentative, and destructive were likely to have more emotional problems later. A press release from Penn State on his analysis said, "Compared to their better adjusted peers, children with a history of behavior disorders, once they entered adulthood, achieved significantly lower levels of overall happiness, life satisfaction, and self-esteem. They also reported weaker rapport with relatives, poorer relations with their parents, and in general more difficulty establishing intimacy."

Ouch.

Many would argue that these kids have emotional disorders to begin with that remain throughout their lives. Surely that is true for some disturbed children.

But it's a good bet that many of the kids Knoester describes—the ones we see screaming at, arguing with, or disobeying their parents in grocery stores, restaurants, and malls—are simply children whose parents did everything in their power to avoid telling them no. It appears that allowing such behavior to become a habit is so ingrained in many parents and children that they often don't notice the problem until it's way too late.

In *The Epidemic*, Shaw reports on a study from Rhode Island Hospital researchers which examined kids who had sleep disorders. The researchers asked the parents about their child's temperament and behavioral problems. They found that "lax and permissive parenting was strongly associated with sleep disturbances." The researchers described lax parenting as allowing rules to go unenforced, providing positive consequences for bad behavior (such as letting kids stay up when they resisted bedtime), or giving in when they threw a tantrum. That description fits a lot of American parents.

When it comes to our kids, Shaw rightly says, "We're depriving them when we don't say no, not when we do."

The Proof Is in the . . . Pudding?

One in five American children is now clinically obese, and that number is growing fast. Just two decades ago, such a staggering statistic would have been unimaginable. These kids are at risk for a lifetime of debilitating physical problems and early death. Surely this has something to do with the fact that the adult population, too, is getting fatter faster than ever before.

I have also long suspected that the epidemic of obese children in America has to do with parents who won't say no. I mean, they're creating kids who can't imagine denying their appetites for food—or *anything*.

Sure enough, the journal *Pediatrics* reported a most interesting study conducted by University of Michigan behavioral pediatrician Dr. Julie Lumeng and her colleagues at Boston University. The study was controlled for every conceivable variable, from poverty levels to the mother's obesity, and the results were based on the National Longitudinal Survey of Youth, another ongoing federal study of behavior and kids.

The researchers, according to the university press release, "found a clear link between childhood obesity and behavior problems. . . . Children who have significant behavior problems, as described by their parents, are nearly three times as likely to be overweight as other children.

In addition, [normal-weight] children with behavior problems are as much as five times more likely to become overweight later."

When it comes to obesity and behavior problems, we can't say which, if either, *causes* the other. But we can say that getting our kids comfortable with "no" is arguably a health issue, not just a matter of character.

"No" Shouldn't Be a No-No After All

I struggle with denying my children little things that seem so big in my mind. Not just Christmas ornaments they didn't really want in the first place, but things like not letting Peter join his friends to play outside because he has to practice the piano and he can see his friends another time. Or telling my daughter she can't take gymnastics right now because she has other activities and getting her to class would completely swamp the family schedule. Or informing my preschooler that she can't join me running errands—which she loves to do—because I have limited time and too many stops to make.

I keep reminding myself, when such things happen and my kids learn to respond graciously—and especially when they don't respond graciously—that they will live through it. And guess what? They do, and I do, too. These small things are little bits of adversity, and learning to respond to them well are tiny moments of practice that will add up, I hope, to better character, a better heart. They are practice for life.

Most of us want our children to be able to say no to all sorts of things someday—drugs, alcohol, sex, the influence of bad peers, temptations that might draw them away from pursuing worthy goals and dreams, the wrong lifetime mate, even greed and laziness. But if we treat "no" as something unworthy, how will our children ever learn to honor it themselves? How will they come to see it not as something ugly but as something that can be good and protective?

Certainly, there are times when it's helpful to distract a child after telling her no. It's good for all of us to learn not to brood on our disappointments. And sometimes an appropriate explanation that a child is old enough to understand is helpful, not to justify a no or win him to your way of thinking at that moment, but to help him learn something from seeing you make a good choice on his behalf.

More important, I am not suggesting that a child shouldn't be able to appeal a no. In fact, teaching them how to appropriately do so makes it clear to them that we understand they are dignified human beings, with all sorts of thoughts and feelings, and that we aren't perfect—or unyielding. Once our children have learned to respect no, they then can learn how to respectfully approach us over a no. Maybe we tell our child to practice the piano, for instance, and she says, "Sure, Mom," and, while moving toward the piano, adds, "but, you know, I just have two more pages to read in that chapter in my book. May I finish those first?" Maybe we tell our child he can't attend a sleepover at a friend's house. Then he makes a respectful case for why it is he will actually get some sleep and not be exhausted the next day. So then, maybe our no even becomes a yes.

Being able to engage with our kids, to really listen to what they have to say, being able to rethink our nos, or stand by them when it's appropriate, are the fruits a confident parent can enjoy.

In chapter 12, I'll discuss discipline and ways of enforcing no.

My goal here is to help us see that if we want our children to believe that "no" is a positive word, protective of body and soul, we have to start believing it and acting as though we believe it ourselves.

Parenting Check

I sometimes find myself wanting to explain a no to one of my children not because I want my child to understand the good reasons for my choice for her, but because I desperately want to justify it to her. I have to remember that I'm not going to get in response, "Good point, Mom, I hadn't thought of it that way." It may even be that the words I use in the two different instances, whether I'm explaining or justifying, are similar. It's my confidence that will be different. That confidence level will be communicated to my child. The more it's there, the more that puts me in a better position of reaching her heart.

As parents, I think we also have to ask ourselves, Do we believe that no is a good and protective thing? How do we handle the nos in our own life? How do our kids see us handle them?

9

Who Chose to Give Kids So Many Choices?

In an early scene of the delightful 2003 remake of the Disney movie *Freaky Friday*, Jamie Lee Curtis is dropping off her surly fifteen-year-old daughter at school. "Bye, honey," she calls after her. "Make good choices!" The audience in which I sat laughed uproariously. And why not? Though the parenting culture acts as if giving young children choices is the golden ring of parenting, deep down we worry about whether that's such a good idea.

We should. Here's what the parenting culture says about kids and choices. *What to Expect: The Toddler Years* advises: "Giving your [toddler] decision-making opportunities will provide a sense of control now and set her on the road to becoming a wise decision-maker later—though you can expect that, at first, many of her decisions will be far from sage."

The experts at the Public Broadcasting System say under "Whole Child" on their website (pbs.org): "The toddler's drive toward independence and self-assertion is an important state of emotional development . . . provide as many choices for your child as possible . . . when children are expected to choose for themselves what they want to do, they have endless opportunities for making decisions." Finally, "when children don't have opportunities to make choices, endless struggles result with a spirited child and a loss of self-confidence in less spirited children."

Here's what Dr. Sears says about choices and school-age children in his book *The Successful Child:*

> To help our children make wise decisions in their lives, we have always given them the freedom of choice. They make their own decisions regarding a number of things: who their friends are, what activities they do away from home, and how they will approach a large homework assignment. We always discuss possible consequences of their actions and let them know how we feel about what they are doing. But in the end, the decision is theirs to make. As well, the consequences are theirs to learn from.

Parenting.com (the website of *Parenting* magazine) sums up the views of the parenting culture best. The experts there say that by the time a child gets to age three or four, "Above all, she's ready to make decisions." She is?

Decisions, Decisions

One fall day I was the assistant helper at the elementary-school fun fair's Sno-Kone machine. The problem was, I was only the *assistant* Sno-Kone maker. I scooped the shavings into the cones, and another mom, the head Sno-Kone maker, poured the colored syrup. Sounds simple enough, right? Ah, but this loving mom was a product of the parenting culture. As the Sno-Kone line snaked around the gym, stretching to five, ten, twenty, and then thirty kids long, she insisted on giving every child his preference among any or all of five different syrups. Green, orange, red, yellow, and blue? "Sure." Green, red, blue, in diagonal stripes? "Absolutely, dear." "Green, red, blue, no, um, orange and—no wait— um, okay, I'm not sure." And so it went.

Meanwhile, children were waiting in line more than twenty minutes to get a Sno-Kone made to their exact specifications. And all for what? So the kids could mix colors for the heck of it, not because they had any real preference. Sno-Kone coloring for grins might have been no problem— but not when doing so kept dozens of children unnecessarily waiting in line while they missed the fun fair *and* kept who knows how many more from getting a Sno-Kone at all when they gave up on the long line.

My idea? Allow one color choice until the line went down or, better yet, make a lot of grape cones and say, "We're serving grape right now. Come back in ten minutes and we'll have lime." Let's face it. If we had handed out nothing but cherry Sno-Kones, the kids would have loved it and been totally satisfied. But this mom would have none of it. She was adamant that we fulfill every child's wish, allow every child to make his or her own decision, no matter how it held up the works for everyone else. Next year, I'm going to be in charge of that Sno-Kone machine!

Even the parenting culture says kids shouldn't be allowed to make decisions about everything. But that's where these experts turn themselves into pretzels.

Here's what I left out of the quotes above: the folks at PBS add, "But not everything is a choice, and sometimes the answer is 'no.' There are many choices that you can offer, but they are limited choices: not 'do you want to put on a sweatshirt?' but 'which sweatshirt?' Not 'do you want any vegetables on your plate?' but 'do you want carrots or beans?'"

The authors of *What to Expect* add, "When she makes a less-than-perfect choice, spare her the 'I told you so's' and let it speak for itself . . . for example, she insists on wearing a dress to the playground and then falls and scrapes her knee. Instead of 'I told you to wear pants . . . ,' try 'I'm sorry you scraped your knee. What do you think you can do next time you come to the playground to keep your knees from getting hurt?'"

This seems to be the paradigm of the parenting culture: children should have as many choices as possible presented to them, because it builds both their autonomy and their all-important self-esteem. Decision making empowers them, and that's how they learn to make good choices. And consequences, even bad consequences (as long as they aren't dangerous), are a good teaching tool. But they shouldn't be allowed to make choices about dangerous or totally inappropriate things, of course.

The problem here is not that there's no sound advice offered; the problem is that there's no principle at work. So we end up with conflicting ideas on the subject of choices, some of which are good, but none of which have any purpose holding them together.

The Consequences of Using Consequences to Teach About Choices

Teaching children about good choices is no longer the job of parents—it has become the job of either natural or logical consequences. These seem to be the cure-all of the experts.

Typically, natural consequences allow the child to learn from the natural order of the world. If he stays up too late, he's tired the next day. If he doesn't put his clothes in the hamper, he doesn't have clean clothes to wear. Logical consequences are consequences the parents generally help to arrange. "If you don't choose to play nicely, we're going home." Usually, when experts teach about consequences and choices, they mean natural consequences, whereas logical consequences are typically used for matters of discipline. (More on that later.) Either way, here's where the parenting culture may be particularly naive.

Some experts seem to see consequences as the Rosetta stone of bringing up baby. In *The Discipline Book,* Dr. Sears says, "Experiencing the consequences of their choices is one of the best ways children can learn self-discipline."

Really? Let's think about that. Too often there are no undesirable natural consequences for bad choices. Sometimes the consequences are delayed; other times, they're simply overwhelming. And even when the natural consequence is something a child might learn from, she often lacks the ability to do so because she lacks the maturity to interpret those consequences correctly.

For example, a parent of a teen might point out, "If you don't want to clean your room, it's your choice. But then you'll reap the consequences of a messy, disorganized living space." What if the teen says, "Great"? The teen may perceive this as a choice with no undesirable consequences, and in fact the real consequences may be delayed for decades before his sloppy habits, which have seeped into other areas of his life, finally begin to cause problems.

A child might learn that if she "chooses" not to play with her little brother, her little brother eventually stops trying to be included. Aha! A natural consequence of her actions but not an undesirable one from her perspective, and therefore not a bad choice. But the delayed consequence that she can't grasp now is how her actions might ultimately affect her friendship with her brother. More important, she's missed an important moral lesson in being kind to others.

Despite the advice in *What to Expect*, I would not let my three-year-old wear a dress to the park to teach her a lesson. That's ridiculous. Can a three-year-old grasp that it was her decision that caused the skinned knee? Imagine a child with the maturity to work backward from the undesirable effect to the decision she made. Assume that she can accept with equanimity that her decision caused the problem and can get to the point where she understands: "Mom, you were so right. I should have put pants on. I'll remember this next time." Isn't this a child who could have accepted wise guidance before she wore the dress? And have you ever actually met a three-year-old like this?

Or, consider the child who helps a friend who is being bullied and himself becomes hurt in the process. By the rules of natural consequences, he *shouldn't* have helped his friend. Is that what we want him to learn? What about a child who cheats on a test and isn't caught? What does he learn when there are no natural consequences? And if he confesses to relieve the guilt in his heart, he will probably experience some pretty bad natural consequences for making that moral choice. But contrary to the laws of natural consequences, it will still have been the right thing to do.

The Moral and the Practical (and Why the Difference Matters)

Yes, I think there are instances when parents should allow their child to experience the natural consequences of a bad choice. That's an important lesson in learning how the world works, which is a necessary part of growing up. Here's how I make the distinction: Is the matter at hand an ethical issue or just a practical one? I am not going to allow a choice on a clearly moral issue: lying, deliberately hurting others, disrespecting me, willfully ignoring a homework assignment or shirking a responsibility, and so on. I also think there are a lot of issues where a parent and his child's views may differ, say in dress or music, but a clear moral issue is *not* at stake. (More on that in chapter 11, "Led Zeppelin and the Culture Wars.")

So, for instance, I wouldn't approve of my fourth-grader deliberately turning in a truly sloppy homework assignment, because not doing his best is not a good moral choice, even if there is some sort of a consequence for it in class. (I might very well make him do that assignment over.) But if that same child forgot his homework assignment, unless it was on purpose, it wouldn't be a moral issue. I might not run it to school for him, just to teach him a practical lesson about how the world works—and that he has to be more responsible. (Full disclosure—again. I have more than once hustled homework assignments and lunches and jackets and forms and money and you name it to school. Worse: I recently had a carelessly forgotten homework assignment FedExed to us on vacation so it could be completed on time. Sigh.)

I might let Victoria, who wants to play all afternoon and do her piano lessons and homework later, experience the consequences of that choice. Doing homework and piano lessons after dinner is not inherently immoral. And having her experience a few evenings of trying to cram it all in—if I thought she'd walk away with the right understanding—might teach her a practical lesson about letting work pile up and then trying to do it all at once.

I would also have to be as sure as I could be—and there are no guarantees—that the child would be mature enough to grasp the implications of making a poor choice and failing to make a good one. Or at least I'd have to believe that the failure would cause the child to mature in some way. Most important, along the way I would ask myself: Am I helping to build a humble spirit into my child so that he or she is willing to learn from mistakes?

I am not going to agonize endlessly over every decision, over every choice. My family would be paralyzed if I did. So I have at times said to each of my kids, for instance, "I don't care if you can't find matching shoes—just choose two things to put on your feet that look more or less the same, *right now,* and get into the car—we have to go!" (This, of course, speaks to lessons about not putting things where they belong, one of my own personal best faults.)

But generally I try to distinguish: Is the matter at hand a practical one, in which natural consequences might teach my child something about how the world works, or is it a moral question, in which natural consequences cannot reach his or her heart?

Children Learn to Make Wise Choices by Having Wise Choices Made for Them

A very wise mom once put it this way to me: "Children do not learn to make good choices by making choices. They learn to make good choices by having good choices made on their behalf."

For Victoria's fourth birthday, I had the bright idea of celebrating by taking five little ones to a busy children's theme restaurant. You know, one of those places with a jungle scene the kids love and horrible food the adults find inedible. Before the waiter arrived, I had told the kids, "I'm going to order for you, so we can order quickly and not hold up the busy waiter." When the waiter got to the table—looking rather nervous, I thought—I ordered a grilled cheese sandwich and a Sprite for each child. (Note to the food police: My children rarely get sodas instead of milk.) The waiter was stunned and profusely thankful. He was expecting, "I want the grilled cheese . . . no, I want the hot dog like Mary's having. I don't want a Sprite, I changed my mind, I want a Coke, too!"

Now a four-year-old may well be able to choose between a grilled cheese sandwich and a hot dog. But for five children to do so would have inevitably delayed the waiter and the other patrons. Though in many ways this was a practical matter, it had moral implications, as seemingly simple choices often do—in this case consideration of others. These kids were too young to understand that on their own and to act accordingly.

But seeing the whole picture, I was able to step in, make good decisions on their behalf (okay, so the Sprite might not qualify, but it *was* a birthday party), and set a good example. The children were happy, and none of them questioned the fact that the food decision had been made. So often it seems that when kids know what the program is, they are positively relieved to go along with it.

Previous generations have understood what is still an obvious truth, if we care to see it: children are not born with wisdom. Wisdom is gained only through experience or through the experience of watching or learning from others and being able to apply that experience to ourselves. These things require maturity, and they require parents, and other adults, who are willing to properly interpret such experiences for children.

A friend of mine is an expert rafter. One summer, he was on a trip with other longtime rafters and an experienced guide. They had not gone down this particular river before, but of course the guide had, many times. At the outset, she told the rafters, "You must trust my commands. When we get into white water, do as I say and we'll be fine." When they reached a particularly turbulent section of white water, the guide called out for the rafters to bear left. It looked as though they should bear right instead, but they followed her instructions, because she was the guide and it was her job to get them down the river safely. As they came around the bend, they could see clearly that bearing right would have driven them straight into some enormous rocks. They had understood that their guide was the expert and had followed her directions, even when their instincts told them otherwise—even when, left to themselves, they would have chosen differently.

Another time, the guide might say, "Here you may bear right if you want to see the scenery, or left if you want to go through some rapids." The rafters would understand that she was giving them a choice *under her wise purview* and within boundaries that would keep them safe.

We used to have the understanding that parents were like that river guide. Now, it seems, our culture has completely flipped on this issue. Today we see choices as kids' inherent birthright and empowerment as their natural heritage. As a result, for Mom and Dad to contravene that understanding and to step in to make choices for them, asserting their authority, is an unpleasant chore to be undertaken only when necessary for the preservation of life and limb. (This is similar to the idea of "no" being inherently unpleasant, as discussed in chapter 8.)

So the parenting culture says to give your child choices whenever you can but not about really big things that could hurt him. The problem, of course, is that a child who is used to making choices all day long sees that as his prerogative and is going to balk when he's not allowed to make a big decision. From his perspective, why can't he decide not to take his medicine? Why can't he decide what websites to visit on his own? Why can't he decide whether to obey Mom and Dad? To his inexperienced mind, no matter how bright he is, there's no context in which he can understand that some decisions are okay for him to make and others aren't.

The only way for a child to make sense of this otherwise conflicting notion is to grasp the principle behind it—that his choices, rather than being his birthright, come at his parents' loving discretion.

Of course, why on earth should kids understand this when so many *adults* don't?

My family loves to ski. All my kids learned to ski at a young age, and they're crazy about it. One year we went to a ski resort in California for a week. Before our trip, I called the ski area to make reservations for ski school. My two older kids got squared away easily, but Madeleine, who was just weeks away from her fourth birthday, presented a problem. "If they're under four they have to choose to ski," the ski-school representative told me.

"Huh?" I asked. "What does that mean?"

"Well, we don't take them outside unless they want to go. It's entirely up to them." I thought to myself, If Maddie wants to pay the bill it's up to her. Meanwhile, it's up to me. But the ski school was adamant: it had to be her choice. Ben asked me, "Does Maddie have to actually initiate the subject of skiing? Or can the ski school at least broach the idea to her?"

I didn't think these people could be serious. They were. Ben and I put her in ski school and said, "We want her out there on the hill," only to come back later in the day to find her watching videos and eating Rice Krispies treats. We asked if she had been out. Well, the instructor said, not really. She had wanted to stay inside.

From our little one's point of view, it was a totally rational decision, an obvious choice with clear consequences. She could either stay warm inside, eating Rice Krispies treats and watching videos, or go out on that cold hill with boards on her feet and risk falling down. Given what she knew in that almost-four-year-old brain of hers, she was making a good choice.

Could she have any idea that she was missing a lot of fun and the chance to learn a skill that would build her self-confidence and give her something in common with her family? No. Now, if she had gone out and tried it, only to dissolve into tears of frustration, I would have said, sure, bring the poor kid inside. I was not looking for a Nazi-like ski school. I just wanted her out on the hill, getting used to the basics of skiing and having some fun before going in for hot chocolate.

But the school didn't have her even try! Nor were the folks there concerned that her mom and dad wanted her to try. The ski-school teacher seemed amazed that we thought our choice should count more than our preschooler's.

I found it particularly baffling that the seven-year-olds couldn't choose whether or not to ski—if they were in ski school, that's what they had to do. So an almost-four-year-old was given a choice, but an older child who presumably had more knowledge about the situation was not. I mean, how mixed up is this whole "kids and choice" thinking?

We took Maddie out of that ski school and put her in one on a different, nearby mountain. She took a class with a ski instructor from Argentina who apparently was not familiar with America's parenting culture. Without giving her a choice, he had her out on the hill learning to ski—and she loved it! By the end of the trip, she was skiing with the family on easy trails, and she couldn't have been happier or more proud of herself.

There was no way our little girl could have made a responsible choice not to ski, so we did not allow her to make that choice. The first ski school seemed to think that letting a child make a choice was so important that no one could intervene, except perhaps in extraordinary circumstances, to make a good choice on the child's behalf. Too bad for all the other potential little skiers whose moms and dads let them make the choice not to ski.

Explaining vs. Justifying

Once kids understand the principle that choices are a privilege, not a right, and once parents really believe that kids learn best by having wise choices made for them—and what kinds of choices kids should and shouldn't be making to begin with—that's when parents can most effectively begin to turn appropriate choices over to their kids.

A big first step in the process is explaining our choices, when it seems appropriate, but not justifying them. A mother who explains to her three-year-old that stripes don't go with plaid so the child may not wear that combination has a better chance of being able to successfully turn over some clothing choices when the child is six.

If a father says to a six-year-old, "We're going to spend the day with Grandma. She's not feeling well, and going there instead of going to your cousin Bobby's house again will cheer her up," it's more likely that that child, when ten years old, will make good choices when faced with situations calling for empathy.

Explaining isn't simply sharing information. It should send the message, "I love you, I am wiser than you, and I have authority in your life." And within those parameters, "Here's why I made the choice that I did." As your child watches someone he knows and trusts make good decisions on his behalf, he can begin to internalize that "character compass" and learn to make more and more good decisions on his own.

Of course, the parenting culture is wild about explaining choices to kids—to ridiculous extremes. The difference between them and me may be a matter of degree and purpose.

Take diapers. I typically bought the packs of disposable diapers with pictures of various animals on them. When Olivia was two, she came to prefer the diapers in the pack with a picture of a horse. (Yes, I know, diaper preference is a sure sign of toilet readiness, but that's another issue.)

Anyway, that darn horse turned up on only about one in ten diapers. But I know parents who would root around and find the horse diaper every time. Or they would go into a long explanation about why she couldn't have the horse diaper that time. Why? Because they feel that they have to justify themselves to a two-year-old.

I told my daughter, "No horsy diaper this time."

But at least she's expressing a legitimate desire, as opposed to the gratuitous choices so many parents almost force their kids to make. A child may have absolutely no preference between Corn Flakes and Cheerios, but Mom and Dad ask her to choose because they think it's a good idea for her to make choices. All she's really learning is that she's calling the shots for no particular reason other than that her parents want her to. She learns that she's in control of her world even when she has no idea what she's doing.

She is being forced to act in ignorance.

We see the results of this attitude in the adult world all the time. In public opinion polls, for instance, fewer and fewer people are willing to say, "I don't know." From foreign policy to presidential politics, they may have absolutely no idea what they are talking about, but they sure think they are entitled to an opinion. I wonder if a lot of these people were told at age one to choose between Cheerios and Corn Flakes when they couldn't have cared less what actually ended up in their cereal bowl.

So, first, I ask myself: Does my child really have enough experience with these different things to have a legitimate preference? Often, the answer is yes.

For example, Olivia loves wearing dresses. Apparently, she finds them more comfortable and easier to move around in than pants or play-suits. She always asks for a dress and, when it's appropriate, I let her wear one. When my other daughters were her age, they didn't care whether they wore pants or dresses, so I didn't offer them those clothing choices; I simply dressed them and left it at that.

Likewise, when Maddie was four, she preferred *The Wiggles* to *Tele-tubbies* (which, as far as I'm concerned, makes a great deal of sense). Victoria prefers pigtails to a ponytail. I like ponytails better, but she likes the way she looks in pigtails. When I have time, I'm happy to do pigtails for her. Meanwhile, Peter prefers golf to playing the piano . . . though he still has to do both. These are all legitimate preferences my children have. When practical, I'm happy to indulge them.

On the other hand, I've fallen into the trap of giving silly choices myself countless times. Sometimes it just seems easier at the moment. Sometimes it is. And I suppose my kids aren't going to be permanently damaged if I say, "Okay, everybody, make your own breakfast—I'm swamped today," or if I give in to Pete when he wants to go to a friend's house although I'd really rather he go to the pool with the rest of us, for instance.

And yes, I have actually stood in front of a TV set on a Saturday morning endlessly switching channels for a three-year-old until I found something that suited her fancy at that moment. It happens, okay? Been there, done that.

I've also done the ultimate dumb thing, and more than once: I've suggested to four children on a Saturday afternoon, "Let's go to a movie. What do you kids want to see?" Or, "We're going out to eat tonight—where would you like to go?" Of course, I get four different answers *and* the bonus of a fight breaking out. Especially at those times, I remind myself, again, that my kids *will* live if they are not offered choices at every conceivable opportunity. Still, I at least try to think through what I'm doing in giving my child choices.

As choices get more complicated, it's not always enough just to have a preference and have it make sense. Our children have to have gained the breadth of knowledge they need to intelligently make the choice at hand—to see it in its larger context. Chocolate over carrots might be a real preference and, in a way, it makes sense. But before being allowed to make a choice, kids have to be able to understand the consequences of that choice. Eating chocolate instead of carrots, over time, is going to have some pretty nasty health consequences.

I'm sure Peter would not have chosen to take piano lessons. He certainly wouldn't choose to practice five or six days a week. He'd much prefer video game time. But he does not have that choice because, as I've explained to him, I am giving him the gift of music. It will be a joy to his soul throughout his life, I explain, but he cannot understand that now. Yet, over the years he's been studying piano, he's progressed into some complicated pieces that even now bring him satisfaction. He's beginning—just beginning—to see what a good choice playing the piano is, though it was a choice he never would have made for himself. What a lesson he's learning about choices.

Most important, I think, our goal should be to have our child get to the place where she understands the impact of her choices on others. When she can rightly see and appreciate and care about the consequences of that choice for those around her, not just for herself, that's when she is in the best position to make a wise choice.

It's actually very hard for young children to even understand that choosing one option means forgoing another. Developmentally, it's difficult for them to grasp that saying yes to the ice cream means that the chocolate cake is literally off the table. In fact, as Neil Swidey of the *Boston Globe* explained it, MRI studies have shown that teens (and so one can probably assume children, too) use different parts of their brains to make decisions from those adults use. They are governed by the emotional parts of their brains, whereas we adults tend to use the areas of our brains related to planning and judgment to make decisions. In other words, we parents really are better equipped to make decisions than our kids are. What's sad is that one needs to justify such an obvious truth.

Anyway, let's not forget that the responsibility inherent in so many choices can put a lot of stress on the shoulders of a little one. "Do you want to go to Grandma's today or spend time with your cousin Bobby?" is more than a four-year-old should have to handle. They just cannot process that question or think about it in a larger context, so why ask them to?

Most of all, to revisit what I touched on earlier, children do not understand their own moral needs well enough to make choices in that arena, though I see them being allowed to do so all the time: "I can't make my school-age child go to church. He just doesn't want to." "I can't tell him I don't want him running all over the neighborhood with that troublemaker Jimmy. He's really taken with him." "I just can't seem to get him be nice to his grandmother. That kid just likes being rude sometimes."

These are choices a child should not be allowed to make. But if the child sees making choices as his right, instead of a privilege at his parents' loving discretion, he will likely only make more and more such bad decisions. Including choosing whether or not to obey and respect his parents. And that's dangerous.

Because I'm the Mom

There are times when I say, especially to my youngest two kids, "Because I'm the mom and I said so," just as that river guide essentially said, "Because I'm the guide and I said so." Sometimes—many times—there just isn't an explanation, or there isn't an explanation that is appropriate for them or that they can possibly grasp or that would benefit them. But if they have come to understand that, as their parents, we not only have authority but are trustworthy, "I'm the mom and I said so" will carry the moral weight that it certainly should. And it will help to protect our kids.

My children love it when they "talk me into" something; for example, candy at the movie theater. I might say, "Come on, guys, I don't want to get candy this time." They reply, "Mom . . . but we haven't had candy in a long time"—typically meaning about three days—"and it's such a treat. Please, Mom?" So once again I might say, "Well . . . okay."

I'll often add, "You kids wear me down! I can't take it anymore. I give up!" They laugh hysterically. Why? Because at some level they know, even when I give in on something like the candy, that the "giving in" is at my discretion. That I'm giving them a privilege; they are not exercising a right. And that makes a world of difference in their lives and in our relationship.

Too many parents, it seems, reverse this approach. Think of an inverted pyramid, wide at the top, narrow at the bottom. It's a symbol of the way many children are raised today. Their loving parents want to raise them "right," so they listen to all the expert advice that tells parents to rarely limit their children. Their children start life at the wide part of the pyramid.

Experts have encouraged parents to give their little ones freedom and choices at every conceivable opportunity, or to trick their kids into thinking they are being given a choice even when they aren't. But, of course, the children don't learn how to handle freedom; they learn little more than that they're calling the shots.

Flash forward to the teen years, when many parents finally realize that not only is the world a dangerous place but that children can be a danger to themselves. Often the parents panic and want to start restricting their teenager. From clothes to friends to curfews to activities, the parents might try to narrow the pyramid. But by then the child is used to being in charge and making his own choices—he's come to see it as his "right"—so restrictions are often a losing battle.

At some level, parents may recognize this truth. In 2002, more than 80 percent of parents, according to an opinion poll by Public Agenda, a public-opinion research agency in New York, said they think parents of teens must, reluctantly or otherwise, give their kids more freedom. But what's trained them to be ready for that freedom?

Now imagine a real pyramid where, of course, the top is narrow. The child's choices and autonomy are limited. The child is born into the world free to be a child, because her loving parents understand that she doesn't have the capacity, life experiences, or maturity to make most choices for herself. As her parents, that is their job. This child will learn from having wise choices made on her behalf and from having those choices explained—not justified—to her when appropriate. She will come to view the choices she is allowed to make as a privilege, not a right.

Along the way, her parents widen the "freedom pyramid" as they engage with her about the choices they make for her. Under their guidance, they allow her to make choices for herself as they see her wisely handling that privilege. Instead of being enslaved by her passions and encouraged to act in ignorance because she's been trained to be the "choice maker," even when it comes to things she knows or cares nothing about, she can instead act more and more reflectively and thoughtfully.

Such guidance can lay the groundwork for staying connected with children during the teenage years in a way that trying to assert parental authority too late—or just giving up on it altogether—can never do.

The number-one area in which parents said they were failing, according to the Public Agenda poll, is in teaching children to have "self-control and self-discipline," even though an overwhelming number of parents said these character traits are crucially important.

Maybe on some level these parents sense that, by giving kids so many choices they can't possibly be prepared to make, they are letting their kids down when it comes to their rescue mission for their hearts.

I think it's that irony that causes audiences to burst out laughing when they hear the well-meaning mom in *Freaky Friday* say to her teenager daughter, "Bye, honey. Make good choices!"

Parenting Check

I suggest watching your family for a few days, and monitoring what kind of choices you give your kids and what kind of choices they ask for. In general, do you think kids learn more from making choices or from having wise choices made on their behalf? On the whole, would you say your kids see making choices as a privilege or as their right? Which view do you want them to have if you are going to best pursue your rescue mission for their hearts?

10 Feelings, Wo-oh-oh Feelings . . .

So the 1970s song goes. It's become something of a caricature, often prompting simulations of the gag reflex. But feelings are alive and well in our culture. In fact, they have come to rule the culture. Today we believe that we have little control over our emotions. We fear that if we do try to control or direct them, we might become repressed. Above all else, we dare not judge feelings and emotions.

This is just as true in parenting as everywhere else. Here are some tidbits from the experts:

"Validate your toddler's feelings . . . even if they include such negative and difficult-to-handle emotions as jealousy and anger."—From *What to Expect: The Toddler Years*

"Children need to have their feelings accepted and respected," and "All feelings can be accepted, certain actions must be limited."—From *How to Talk So Kids Will Listen and Listen So Kids Will Talk*

"In regards to 'negative' emotions, parents will need to utilize the tool of 'separating the deed from the doer.' This tool allows parents to demonstrate acceptance of all emotions but set limits on inappropriate behavior."—Family counselor and parent educator Ron Huxley (cpirc.org)

"It is important to help children deal with their feelings. . . . Parents can help children express their feelings in ways that will not hurt themselves or others. Children (and adults) need to know that feelings are different from actions. Feelings are always okay—they are never right or wrong. What we do, on the other hand, might be appropriate or inappropriate."
—From *Positive Discipline for Single Parents*

Feelings are *never* right or wrong? I'm going to go out on a limb here. I think Hitler's hatred of Jews was wrong. Moreover, it was his feelings that led to Nazi atrocities. It's naive, or downright foolish, to think that feelings and behavior wholly at odds with each other can exist together for very long. Sure, there are circumstances in which they do, like kissing up to a boss you hate in order to keep your job. Then again, the minute you have a chance at a new or better job, you're gone.

Human beings are just not built to sustain dramatic dissonance between emotions and behavior over the long term.

Still, the entire focus on feelings in the parenting culture is only about the appropriate *expression* of feelings. The focus is almost never on the feelings themselves, nor on the idea that some feelings are not okay or that some feelings may need to be reconsidered, because they're a clue that our hearts are not okay, even if these feelings don't always lead to unwholesome, dangerous, or malicious behavior.

Feelings and the Heart

Reality check: feelings and emotions flow from the heart. Sometimes they're a simple expression of our humanity—an unavoidable, natural response. We hear a noise in the middle of the night, and we bolt upright with terror. (I do, anyway.) Or a driver whizzes down the street where our children are playing, and we feel furious at the driver and protective of our children at the same time. But sometimes feelings reflect what's happening in our hearts. And if we're on a rescue mission for our children's hearts, it's there we often have to go when it comes to feelings.

In the Bible, King David was someone who had profoundly deep, even tormented, emotions. This was not a fellow who believed in a stiff upper lip. He knew that feelings were important and, in his Psalms, he regularly poured them out before God. But David explored his feelings in part to gauge the wholesomeness of his heart and to check those emotions before truth, which is where he found his comfort. Consider Psalm 25:16–21, in which David cries out to God:

> Turn Yourself to me, and have mercy on me, for I am desolate and afflicted, the troubles of my heart have enlarged. Bring me out of my distresses! Look on my affliction and my pain, and forgive all my sins. Consider my enemies, for they are many, and they hate me with a cruel hatred. Keep my soul and deliver me. Let me not be ashamed, for I put my trust in You. Let integrity and uprightness preserve me, for I wait for You.

At times, David was a deeply troubled man, but he wisely recognized that his troubled heart was partly due to his sins, not just his enemies. He wanted his powerful emotions to be weighed against the truth of integrity and uprightness. He knew that an objective assessment of these things, not his strong emotions or even his ability to "express them appropriately," would preserve him. This was not a man who stifled his emotions. Nor, on the other hand, did he think, Everything I'm feeling is okay because I'm me—I just need to really feel good about sharing my feelings!

Those opposite ends of the spectrum seem to be the extremes in parenting today, though the pendulum has definitely swung toward the latter. There may be parents who consistently say, or at least think, "I don't care how you feel. Deal with it." But far more commonly, it appears today's parents want to understand, delve into, and of course accept as legitimate and appropriate every feeling their child has—as long as he shares his feelings in a constructive way.

But just as David recognized that a troubled heart could sometimes come from sin, so must we help our children learn that some of their feelings may come from a heart wrongly oriented. Even when our emotions don't come from malice or ill will, it is helpful to think about them clearly and understand what they are telling us about our hearts, our minds, and our relationships.

So, like the parenting culture, I'm all for helping children better handle and communicate their frustration, confusion, excitement, or disappointment—their feelings. But, not just so they can get something off their chest or feel better. Those might be fine things, but I see listening to what's going on in our children's hearts as the way to learn about the well-being of their hearts. As a way to help guide those hearts for the good.

Sometimes Anger Is Not Okay

Unfortunately, it's not unusual to hear the experts tell us to ignore, or try to understand, or even accept, nasty feelings in a child. So, for instance, it's common to hear that if a child is telling you she hates you, or glaring at you with the evil eye, well, just let her resolve her feelings in another room.

But if a child is glaring with hatred at her parent, that feeling is very likely coming from a troubled heart that needs to be engaged, to be checked against integrity. So there are times when I've told my older kids, "It's not okay to be furious with me, honey. I'm on your side here. I'll be glad to help you better understand that, but you have to put that anger aside."

Once, when Madeleine was two, I actually tried to appease her anger at me (over what issue I now forget) by giving her a piece of chocolate, which she absolutely loves. Yes, let the record show that I have tried to assuage wholly unwarranted anger in a two-year-old with sugary food. Talk about a weak moment! Anyway, she took the chocolate. But, still furious with me, and glaring at me with all-out defiance and making sure I was watching her, she marched over to the wastebasket and threw the chocolate into it with all her might. Although she was already extremely verbal at the time, she didn't say a word. She didn't have to. "Ha!" she was letting me know. "That's what you can do with your chocolate!" So much for my appeasement offering. (And let *that* be a lesson.)

I was so dumbstruck that she would part with a piece of chocolate that I offered no response. (Okay, another weak moment. It was a bad day.) A few minutes later, when she thought my back was turned, I caught her out of the corner of my eye digging furiously through the trash, her chubby arms madly searching that garbage can in a frenzied

effort to retrieve that piece of lost chocolate. At that point, I was doubled over in laughter, though trying hard to conceal it, and couldn't do
much of anything.

But think about what was going on in that heart. She was so angry at
me, and so eager to make a point of that anger, that she was willing to
separate herself from something she desperately wanted—a piece of
chocolate—just to spite me. She was two, not ten, and there were some
simple issues of maturity involved. And the whole episode, on one level,
makes for a good laugh. But on another it showed me something of what
that heart was capable of, even at that tender age.

What I should have done, for starters, was *not* to try to appease anger
with food (duh). Instead, I should have gotten down on one knee, gently
held her arms as I looked her in the eye, and said, "Honey, it is not okay
to be angry with Mom right now." Those lessons need to start early and
simply.

The Orientation of the Heart

Consider the same situation with two different heart orientations: if my
child says, "Mom, I'm upset that you wouldn't let me play video games
when Phillip was here. How come you wouldn't?" or, "Mom, you kind
of embarrassed me at Melanie's house—could you please never, ever
again tell anybody else about the time I [fill in the blank]."

Respectfully approaching me hoping to resolve an issue or letting me
know they wish I'd do something different next time is great. There is
no malice or ill will in their heart. But, if they were to approach me in
heated anger on those same issues, perhaps furious that I had "wronged"
them, I would have to say, "Sorry, darlin', what's going on right now in
that heart of yours is not okay. When you can think rightly about
approaching me, then we can talk about it."

It's very often the case that the issue at hand isn't the feeling, say frustration or irritation, or even anger. We don't have to whitewash our feelings. At times any of those sentiments might, in fact, be quite appropriate. The issue is the disposition of the child's heart in dealing with those feelings.

When I started to write this book, I wrote with some relief that I've never had one of my children express "hatred" for another (or for me). That's since been overtaken by events. I've let the children involved know that that is absolutely unacceptable, because even if just for a moment, such sentiments mean malice and ill will are in their hearts.

On the other hand, one of my kids might say, "Mom, I'm so frustrated with Olivia right now—can you please keep her from getting into my schoolwork?" Well, there's no malice there. And I might be able to take away the frustration by moving Olivia away from the schoolwork.

It comes down to the child's heart, and what's going on in there as they deal with their feelings.

By the same token, if Peter saw one of his little sisters being bullied or hurt by an older child, I would expect him to have anger in his heart—not malice toward the bully, but appropriate anger—and to take steps to help her. In that case, my son's anger would be wholesome and would arise out of his love for his sister.

Helping our children think about what's going on in their hearts as they experience a variety of emotions and measure what's going on there against integrity and goodness is part of our rescue mission for them. When we don't do this for them, we rob them of part of the beauty of their humanity.

Poison

And so, contrary to what the parenting culture teaches, there are some feelings to which it would be helpful to develop a natural, protective aversion at all times. Most parents will tell their children to back off from rusty nails and strangers, among other things. Our children might not naturally do so if we didn't help them develop a protective revulsion when it comes to these things. So, too, I've told my children that feelings like hatred, resentment, bitterness, and jealousy are poison to the heart.

When Madeleine, at age four, figured out what the word "poison" meant and understood that I considered some feelings poisonous, the color drained from her face. "Really, Mom? They're really poisonous?" Well, no, I told her, not in the sense that they would necessarily make her physically sick, though I suppose they could, but that they could make her soul sick—and that was worse!

In his book *The Progress Paradox*, sociologist Greg Easterbrook discusses a new area of study, "forgiveness research," and reports that "people who do not forgive the wrongs committed against them tend to have negative indicators of well-being, more stress-related disorders, lower immune system function, and worse rates of cardiovascular disease than the population as a whole."

Yep, poison.

This does not mean we have to forgive in the sense of, "Gee, that's fine. It's okay that you caused me so much pain," or that we don't pursue lawful remedies when appropriate, or view sin as sin. It does mean that we don't hold on to a grudge or seek revenge. When we can decide to let it go and move on—we rid ourselves of real poison.

The irony is that the "all feelings are fine" view that our therapeutic nation has adopted minimizes the richness and complexity of emotions.

Understanding our feelings can give us great insight into our emotional makeup, into the very thing that makes us all wonderfully human and unique. But today we no longer learn to think—yes, *think*—rightly about our feelings and emotions. We don't teach our children to reflect on their feelings. We are certainly loath to make—gasp!—value judgments about our feelings. When it comes to feelings, the only thing that is frowned upon in our culture today is not sharing them enough with the world. We are, it seems, slaves to our feelings. Reducing our agency as human actors surely minimizes our humanity.

I Don't Care If You Don't Feel Like Eating Fish

I hardly have my kids' feelings under a microscope every minute. In fact, there have been times when I've told my kids that their feelings don't matter. Because the world does not—thankfully—revolve around them or their feelings at any one moment. If they say, "I don't feel like eating fish for dinner," I'll likely say, "I don't care how you feel about it, you're eating it." Or if they say they don't feel like practicing the piano, I might say, "Of course you don't feel like it, but that doesn't matter. You have to do it."

There might be other times to talk to them about how I choose good meals for them or how music will bring joy to their souls over time. But sometimes our kids just need to get the job done, and they have to have a good attitude about it even if they don't feel like it at the moment. Simply because, as we say in our home, "attitude is everything."

Other times, say in dealing with something like sadness, we might just need to say, "I'm sorry the neighbor kids kicked over your dollhouse, honey. Here, let me help you fix it back up." In other words, acknowledge it, don't dwell on it, and turn the child's thoughts to happier ones.

If my child is brooding because her sister is playing with someone else that day or is disappointed over not making the school play, it's appropriate to let her express those things and to sympathize. Then, at some point (typically sooner rather than later), I simply say, "Honey, you need to move on now." Often parents can willfully redirect their child's attention to something else and so teach the child that sometimes he has to deliberately decide to focus on something more positive than a negative feeling. We all know how very seductive negative feelings can be. We have to help our children learn not to be seduced by them.

The Heart and the Brain

Learning when and how to think about our feelings, and how to think about them rightly, is an incredible gift we can give our kids. This is age-old wisdom. The Apostle Paul wrote, "Whatever is true, whatever is right, whatever is pure, whatever is lovely, whatever is of good repute, if there is any excellence and if anything is worthy of praise, let your mind dwell on these things" (Philippians 4:8). Two thousand years later, it shouldn't really be a surprise that science recommends this, too.

Dr. Jeffrey Schwartz is a widely respected neuroscientist and research professor of psychiatry at the University of California at Los Angeles. In 1997, he made headlines with his book *Brain Lock,* in which he described a revolutionary method for treating obsessive-compulsive disorder (OCD). Schwartz found that by training OCD patients to willfully redirect their thoughts of compulsive urges, he could teach them to refuse to "consent" to the practice of checking twenty times to see if they turned off the iron, for instance. Instead, they learned to "consent" to a healthy behavior such as gardening. Amazingly, changing their behavior changed the way these patients' brains were physically wired.

In 2002, Schwartz published another extraordinary book, *The Mind and the Brain: Neuroplasticity and the Power of Mental Force*, in which he goes a step further and shows that it's not just different behavior that can rewire our brains, but also different thinking.

Remember the classic musical *The Music Man?* Professor Harold Hill cons a small town into buying all kinds of musical instruments for its kids. But Hill can't read a note of music, so he tells the kids to "think" a piece of music—he calls it his patented "think system."

Preposterous, right? Not really. What Schwartz found was that people who only thought about carefully playing a piece on the piano had, over time, the exact same physical changes in their brains (measured by CT scans) as people who actually played the piece on the piano.

In many different experiments he duplicated these results, until he came to the conclusion that it's not "mind over matter" but that "mind changes matter"—or, that deliberately changing the way we think about things can actually change the physical wiring of our brains. And that physical rewiring, in turn, has a huge impact on the way we behave and feel and even think, and so we create a positive upward spiral. Schwartz calls this deliberate redirection of the way we think "mindfulness."

Wow.

His findings have implications for treatment for OCD and depression, as one might suspect, but also for disorders such as Tourette's syndrome and even stroke.

And Schwartz's research can encourage us to help our children think rightly about their feelings. His findings don't dehumanize us or minimize the importance of our emotions. Just the opposite: they mean that we can better assert our humanity by resisting the tendency to become slaves to our passions. We're not just animals after all.

How freeing is that?

As parents, we see our little ones tossed from pillar to post by their emotions. We don't need to treat them as if they were OCD patients, but we *can* help them understand that they are not the sum product of their feelings. We can teach them that they have some ability to govern their feelings, not just their behavior. And because the former so often leads to the latter, this is a gift indeed.

This is not a magic formula that will allow us to constantly control our emotions. Control of our feelings, if it were possible or even a good thing, is not the ultimate goal anyway.

Reflection

Helping our children to reflect rightly on their feelings is what we're after. If we treat all feelings as okay, we lose a chance to reach our children's hearts and help them understand their own hearts better.

So, for instance, take the issue of fairness. Has a child ever demanded fairness because he was really concerned about justice? Um, no. Say one child is invited to a birthday party and another is not. A parent's response might be to share in the uninvited child's sadness and sense of being treated unfairly, while also reminding him how many parties he's sure to be invited to in the future.

I think we need to help our children to think differently. Instead of assuming that one child's good fortune means that the other is "owed" something, how about encouraging the child who was not invited to be happy for the child who was? That's an entirely new and better way of approaching his feelings about the situation. But we're not free to try to get our child to that point if we think we must always accept his feelings just as they are.

I had such a situation on my hands recently. One of my children was getting more and more excited about her upcoming birthday, while her sister's attitude was noticeably deteriorating. I figured out that the problem was the attention the birthday child was getting. When I confronted my other child, she broke down in my arms and cried, admitting how difficult it was that all the attention seemed to be going toward her sister.

I didn't tell that child that her feelings were unimportant, but I also didn't validate what was a sort of childish, though not malicious, selfishness. Nor did I emphasize the obvious: that this child had a birthday once a year, too. I mean, what if she was upset about her sibling getting something I *couldn't* match for her? The moment wasn't right for any really profound points. I just wanted to convince my daughter right then that she was loved and that she would be much happier if she could try—just try—to find a measure of joy in the birthday child's joy.

Can you imagine how much better off we all would be if we could learn that lesson early?

I was glad to have had that insight into her heart, and I told her I was pleased she had told me how she felt. That night, we got only as far as "I know how I feel isn't right, Mom, but it's hard to feel happy about her birthday." That was a good start. She was beginning to learn that I took her feelings seriously and that she had a responsibility to measure them against what was right.

I invited her to shop with me for the birthday child and help pick out some presents that were just right. This gave her a concrete way to share in her sister's joy. The next few days were infinitely better.

Understanding my child's feelings opened a door for me into her soul—but it could be helpful only if I used that door to enter into her heart on my rescue mission.

What Do I Know to Be True?

My younger children frequently ask me what I think about things. Sometimes their questions are about what they should wear for the party or whether I think chocolate or mint chip ice cream tastes better. But sometimes their questions are along the lines of "Where do you think the guy in that car is going, Mom?" or "Do you think the new Harry Potter movie will be better than the first one?" Over and over I explain that thinking requires knowledge. I explain to them that I can't think anything about where the fellow in the car is headed or how I'll rate a movie I haven't seen or heard reviewed, because I have no knowledge about those things.

The idea that having views about something requires some level of knowledge about the issue is not common in our culture. We have a hard time accepting the notion that sometimes we should say, "I don't have enough information to have a legitimate opinion."

My children are learning that they cannot just think whatever they want to about something. Thinking requires understanding. It requires being willing to face the facts, even when we very much wish those facts were different. In other words, we can't just think what we "feel" like thinking.

Let's say a child comes to us terribly offended because the next-door neighbor won't play with her. Our child is hurt. In digging deeper, we discover that the other child couldn't play because she had to do her homework. What matters is that she did not intend to offend our child. So we cannot let our little one wallow in feelings of rejection she ought not to have. Equally important to her perception of what happened is objectively considering the facts. If the other child truly meant no harm, our child must be encouraged not to feel harmed.

Tragically, in our culture the only thing that matters is how we *feel* about a situation. If we feel that we've been a victim, or if we feel that we've been wronged, or if we feel that our boss is unfair to us, what more do we need to know? The art of asking, "Was I actually treated badly?" is a lost one. No wonder depression rates have skyrocketed in recent decades. Being a victim is, well, depressing.

We all know people who hold on to the poison of resentment or bitterness, who continue to wrongly see themselves as victims or too easily take offense when none is meant. Today we have a culture run by feelings. To "think about our feelings" is heard only in the context of "I'll think whatever I want to about my feelings," meaning, "I'll be ruled by them."

I've come to the conclusion that often these people had their emotions either totally ignored or completely validated as children. One thing is a good bet: no one helped them, or even let them know they could, learn to think rightly about their feelings.

In the Psalms, the writer pours out his heart: "Thus my heart was grieved and I was vexed in my mind. I was so foolish and ignorant; I was like a beast before You" (Psalm 73:21–22). In other words, when he didn't think clearly about his feelings, he was as stupid as an animal. It's easy to feel things. It's hard to think about them.

What's Love Got to Do with It?

I'm convinced that one of the most important feelings we don't think rightly about in our culture is *love*. And what a loss that is for our kids!

When we think of that word, we think almost exclusively of warm, tender, or romantic feelings. And those are wonderful, to be sure. But let's face it. Sometimes people—our spouses, our children, and we ourselves—are not "lovable" according to that definition. Tragically, we are so fixated on our narrow definition of love that we may decide that if we don't have those feelings at the moment, we don't love. Countless marriages have ended because one or both partners "lost that lovin' feeling," as the Righteous Brothers put it.

The ancient understanding of love, as is commonly described in the Bible, is so much more meaningful. First Corinthians 13:4–8 is something we often hear read at weddings: "Love is patient, love is kind and is not jealous; love does not brag and is not arrogant, does not act unbecomingly; it does not seek its own, is not provoked, does not take into account a wrong suffered, does not rejoice in unrighteousness, but rejoices with the truth; bears all things, believes all things, hopes all things, endures all things. Love never fails."

Do we ever really think about what that means? It means true love is in the doing.

"To love" should not mean just to feel; it really means to act, to do right by someone, to help someone, to be committed to the object of our love regardless of how we are feeling at the moment.

Many times I've talked to my kids about this: to love is to be committed to doing good unto the other. Conversely, if we say we love someone but disregard that person or treat him or our responsibility to him carelessly, that love is a lie. When I encourage my kids to love one another, I'm not demanding they conjure up warm feelings when their sibling has just broken a favorite toy. I'm encouraging them to do good to the other in spite of the toy-breaking.

Feelings can be like smoke, they may come and go with the wind, but love in action is tangible, and it's much more significant and meaningful for both the giver and the object of that love. Because then it's a choice. It involves the will *and* the heart. It's the fullest expression of our humanity. In other words, for love to mean anything, it has to *do* something. (And so often, making a choice to love encourages the warm feelings to follow.)

When I see a problem brewing with my kids, I'll sometimes ask one of them, "Are you showing your sister love by doing good unto her?"

It's not unusual to have the answer come back, through tightly clenched and very annoyed teeth, "I'm trying, Mom!" That's a start.

We know we can be unlovable at times. Our kids know it, too. So how terrific is it to know that someone is committed to our good, that that person really loves us by deliberate choice and with action—not just smoke and words—even when we know we don't deserve it?

This is not our culture's understanding of love. We give our children a gift when we make it *their* understanding of love.

The Art of the Soul

Have you ever been to an art gallery where you knew very little about the artists or the period? You see complex paintings that mean little to you, and you don't have a way to judge them. Maybe you say, "I sort of like that one better—I think."

But if you put your headphones on and listen to the museum guided tour, suddenly things begin to change. You understand more of the complexity of the paintings, what the artist was trying to communicate, and the different methods or mediums he or she used. Now you can better understand and judge the richness of what you are seeing. That's because you are better able to *think* about the impressions the art makes on you.

Some people say, "There's no good or bad art. There's just art." That's silly. Believing that robs us of the appreciation of art. Our enjoyment of art—or almost anything else, for that matter—increases in direct proportion to our understanding of it and our ability to judge it. The extent to which we don't just let the art wash over us but engage and think about it is the extent to which we can truly enjoy its richness.

In the same way, understanding our feelings and emotions, thinking rightly about them, can guide our hearts for the good. Understanding those things magnifies our humanity. What a gift we can give our children when we help them reflect on their hearts and, as I'll talk about in the next chapter, encourage them to think rightly about their world.

Parenting Check

I think many parents find themselves being most typically "feeling validators" or "feeling ignorers." It helps to know there is another way—to be "feeling thinkers" ourselves, and to help our kids learn to think rightly about their feelings, too.

11 Led Zeppelin and the Culture Wars: The Culture Can Be Cool

I think the rock group Led Zeppelin is fantastic. I want my kids to think so, too. Helping our kids think about their world, about the culture around them, should be a centerpiece of our mission for their hearts.

So I regularly listen to 1960s, '70s, and '80s music with my children. We have a great time crooning along together, and in the process I talk with them about the powerful, throaty romance of Rod Stewart (after all these years I'm still *wild* about Rod Stewart), or the fun of the Beach Boys, or how the music of Simon and Garfunkel touches me to this day. They know that Boston's self-titled album was one of the greatest albums of all time and Led Zeppelin's *In Through the Out Door* was close.

I hope my kids will like my generation's music as well as—maybe even more than—Christina Aguilera and Ashlee Simpson and other modern-day artists (some of whom, I confess, I like, too). It would be great to share musical tastes. But that's probably not going to happen, and that's okay. I want them to at least learn to be discerning about music. To ask themselves, about whatever kind of music they enjoy, "Why do I like this music? Does it move me, or is it just plain fun?" Whether they're profound or just high energy, are the lyrics at least saying *something*? (For the record, they listen to and study classical music, too, so nobody needs to panic.)

I'm not saying that every lyric in these artists' songs is something I want my kids to live by. Nor can I think of any rock stars, past or present, who have personal lives I would want my children to emulate. Not for a minute. I'm not even suggesting that everyone should value rock music as I do. But I am saying that if we think clearly and don't let ourselves be filled with fear of the world, we can find pearls of great value in so many things "of this world." In the Bible, 1 Timothy 4:8 tells us, "For everything created by God is good, and nothing is to be rejected if it is received with thanksgiving."

We need to teach our children how to find what value there is in the things of this wonderful world, and how to distinguish between the good and the bad. More importantly, if we can help our kids to understand that they need to be most engaged when it comes to the battlefield of their heart—even more than the battlefield of the culture—well then, we won't have to be quite so afraid of the world on their behalf.

I think many parents are more fearful of the popular culture, and by extension the world, than they need to be. I'll put it a different way: it's true the world is, generally speaking, a dangerous place, bent on capturing the hearts of our children as I said in the introduction. I just think that often the best way to protect our children from the world is not to try always to shut it out, but to try to help our children to think rightly about it.

In fact, if we try to shut it out, we can miss a lot of the good that *is* in the world.

Some parents want so much to protect their children from the culture that they try to close the world out from their children's lives. But I think that the belief that if only we could shut the world out our children would be safe is naive at best. And not just because the world will find a way to get in anyway. That's true, but it's a cop-out. The issue is that even if we *could* find a way to shut the culture out entirely, sin would still find a way to get into the heart because, as I discussed in chapter 7, "Misbehavior and Other Matters of the Heart," sin comes *from* the heart itself.

So, for instance, I've heard many parents say that they set the "bar" high, so that when children "rebel," they don't really go off the edge. In other words, if we say they can see only G movies, their rebellion is PG. And if rebelling is seeing a PG movie instead of doing drugs, then we're way ahead of the game as parents, right? Obviously, I'd rather have my child watch a movie I'd forbidden than take drugs. But when it comes to the heart, there isn't a huge difference. If our child delights in rebelling against legitimate authority, that's a heart in danger.

There are times and places to shut the world out, or to teach our kids that we do things differently than the world does. Still, the problem is not the world. It's our hearts and their potential to be led astray.

Of course on a host of issues—from music to movies to clothes— our taste, and even our values, may be different from our children's. Dad may be a real-estate developer, while his child becomes an environmental activist. But if we've helped our children to think rightly about many different areas of their lives, to be thoughtful and discerning about their world, those differences won't scare us so much.

I don't want my children to think like me. (Well, okay, I sort of do, but I completely understand that they won't.) What I really want is for my children to be thoughtful, to reflect on their world, their behavior, and their relationships. As they choose friends, for instance, I want them to think about not just how they feel about the person but also about what they think about that person and the friendship. Does this person possess the qualities that make a good friend? And how can my child be a good friend in return?

Which adults do our children admire and look up to, besides Mom and Dad, and why? Are the qualities they admire truly admirable qualities? These are questions we would want our children to consider thoughtfully. If our children admire Britney Spears because she shows her tummy a lot, we should help reorient that thinking.

When we've done our job and taught our children to think carefully about the values they adopt, we don't need to panic when they don't adopt our particular values.

The Whore Wars

Consider the way our children dress. Many of us, particularly parents of girls, are horrified at the outfits that pass for "clothes" in the department stores. Midriff-baring tops and hip-hugger pants for seven-year-olds reflect a culture that sexualizes even its youngest children. The battles parents have with their kids over such clothing have been dubbed "the whore wars." But I'm not sure the "yes or no" battles over clothing get to the heart of the matter. Rather than just argue about what they can and cannot wear, I think it's more important to teach kids that how they dress communicates their values, and how they value themselves.

When my son was in second grade, he had a classmate whose mother obviously believed that how her child dressed was important. Every day, he wore slacks, a button-down shirt, a bow tie, and often a vest. Sadly—and perhaps needless to say—this child was ostracized by the other kids in his classroom. Why on earth did that mother do that to her child?

When I'm invited to a party, one of the first things I do is to ask my friends what they're wearing to the affair. I mean, I don't want to arrive looking like an idiot! So why shouldn't our kids do the same? My daughters and I will, I'm sure, have different tastes in clothes, and each girl will have tastes that are different from those of her sisters. And that's how it should be: individual style is an expression of ourselves.

Rather than try to make my children's style conform to my own taste, I focus on teaching them to think about how their dress reflects their values. If we're invited to Aunt Bev's for dinner, I explain to Peter that he can't show up in slovenly jeans, because he would be sending the message to Aunt Bev, through his clothing, that he doesn't care about her efforts. I might set the parameters—collared shirt and no jeans, for example—and let him take it from there.

And I do have parameters. No baggy, low-slung pants for Pete. No Britney Spears tops for my daughters. I'm teaching them to question their own choices. "With this outfit, am I communicating respect for myself, for my body, for others?" We can have different tastes, but if they're thoughtful about the values they adhere to in their dress, we should be okay.

At the moment, Victoria loves the "girly" look, and dresses more conservatively than I do. Maddie hates dresses; she thinks they are too hard to play in. Olivia wants to wear nothing but dresses. Pete likes the longer shorts and cargo pants that I'm not crazy about, but that I tolerate as long as they are belted around his waist and look neat.

But the bottom line is that I want *them* to think about how they dress. They will and they should develop their own styles—it's a reflection of the individuals they are. If I've helped them think about the values they communicate, I don't have to be afraid of their individual tastes.

Dare Not to Date?

Children and sex and the opposite sex—a flash point in the culture wars.

Years ago, a dear young friend of mine was married. After the reception, the groom's mother told me how thrilled she was that her son's new bride, my friend, was a virgin on her wedding day.

For the record, I firmly believe sex should be saved for marriage—but I hope that if I have this level of information about my children's intendeds, I have the good sense not to share it. In any event, I got the distinct impression that this mother prized virginity above all else. But what if his bride had been malicious or dishonest? Would being a virgin make up for those things? As important as I believe it is to save sex for marriage, if we could secure our children's virginity and yet their hearts were corrupted, we would have failed them.

I wasn't shocked to learn, according to several different news reports, that the vast majority of kids who sign a pledge for "True Love Waits," a national campaign that encourages kids to remain virgins until marriage, fail in their goal. (The good news is that kids who sign the pledge do at least tend to wait longer to have their first sexual experience.) These teens make a promise to God, their parents, and each other to remain celibate. But when I hear these reports, I can't help but worry that so much investment in the act of sex only serves to make it more enticing; forbidden fruit is more appealing.

There is absolutely a place for rules about sexual behavior. And there are many organizations that are great at giving teens the encouragement and the tools they need to say no to premarital sex. But (I know I sound like a broken record, or these days a scratched CD) the older our children get, the more the rules have to be based on helping them learn to think rightly about the world.

I just wonder about the parents of the teens featured in these news articles. So the kids weren't having sex at age sixteen. Good. But why were their parents allowing them to be involved in these intense, exclusive dating relationships to begin with? Why would they think that such a relationship, given all the passion of the teen years even when it *doesn't* involve sex, could be good for a child's heart?

Parents seem divided into camps when it comes to dating: for starters there are those who allow their children to have exclusive dating relationships and cross their fingers that it will not be sexual, and those who are so terrified of their children interacting with the opposite sex that they prohibit any contact at all.

And yes, of course there are parents in the middle. They don't like the idea of intense dating, but they think they have to allow it, that they have no choice. So they set an arbitrary age when their children can date, for example, sixteen. But this doesn't provide any thoughtful framework within which to operate. Why is sixteen magic?

My children are not yet teenagers. But I'm not exactly flying blind here either. I have many wise friends who have successfully raised teens into wonderful adulthood. So I do I know that the lessons we teach our children when they are little will often be what guides them successfully, or unsuccessfully, through those teen years.

That's why I talk with my kids, even now, about how dating doesn't make sense when a person is too young to even think about marriage. Because the feelings and attachments are so intense and the frustrations so great, dating is more likely to make them sad than happy. I tell them that romantic relationships are wonderful when they are ready to think about having the "real deal"—marriage. Even then, I tell them, the best part of marriage is the deep and abiding friendship.

That's one reason I encourage my kids to have friends of the opposite sex. When we lived in Virginia, my girls' best friends were the boys in the neighborhood. No doubt that would have changed in time even if we'd stayed there, but I think that was a wholesome situation. While some of their girlfriends didn't want to come into the neighborhood when the boys were around—they were boisterous, they'd chase, they'd run, they could be rough in the best sense—my girls learned to hold their own around them. I think that's great.

But intense romantic relationships in the teen years? No thanks. I'd be happy to have my daughters escorted to school dances or my son take a girl to such an event, but I'll always oppose pairing off into exclusive couples in the high-school years. Yet I'm not making this some edict that I'll hand down when the "time is right." (That just invites the "forbidden fruit" response.) I'm beginning the discussions now, at a level appropriate for them, hoping to give them a healthy perspective on these things even in these early years.

This is no guarantee that they'll do the right thing when the time comes. But no parent I've ever met wants her young teen to have an intense romantic relationship in high school. We seem to instinctively recognize that nothing good can come of it. I've heard some wise folks say that those early relationships are practice for divorce—not marriage. So just standing back in this area—because I think I *can't* have an impact—seems really nuts.

Friends of mine, parents of four, handled their oldest daughter's teen years admirably. They didn't create an artificial, "you shall not date" regimen or rules about dating when she turned a certain age. From her earliest days, they talked with her, as they have with her siblings since, about the purpose and ideal of marriage, and they modeled it in their own lives.

They encouraged her to enjoy male friendships and pursue academic excellence, sports, and other activities. They helped her see pairing off with a romantic partner as something reserved for marriage. Much more to the point, they helped her to see that anything less than the "real deal" was just an artificial arrangement that was not good enough for her.

There were times in those high-school years when she would go to her dad and say, "Dad, can you tell me again why I'm not dating?" They would even role-play her being asked out and saying no to a one-on-one date. (Group get-togethers were fine, as were one-on-one dates that had a destination point, for example, a homecoming dance.)

This approach will not keep every child from an intense romantic relationship. But the point is not to find a magic formula that keeps children from dating. The point is to persevere with our children and do what we can to reach their hearts. Including reaching their hearts when it comes to encouraging a wonder and appreciation for the great gift of a relationship and all the unique privileges that come with that.

Anything less is abandoning our kids.

Do Kids Really Have a Right to Privacy?

A child's right to privacy has been encouraged, to different extents, by the parenting culture. Or at least it was until Columbine. Now we have to admit that the private lives of children can sometimes be difficult, tormented places.

In 1998, Patricia Hersch wrote *A Tribe Apart: A Journey into the Heart of American Adolescence*. Hersch lived with a group of teenagers right next to the suburb where I once lived. She followed the teens through their lives, becoming amazingly close to many of them and being allowed into their lives in a way that astounds the reader.

What she describes is a life of dangerous privacy. Not just in terms of teens who have telephones, computers, and television sets in their rooms. (Memo to my kids: Not happening—ever.) Not just in terms of teens—whose parents are convinced that "my kids would never do that"—doing drugs. But in terms of teens retreating into a private world, often disconnected from the responsible, discerning adults in their lives. Hersch's book is essential reading for parents.

Hers is a cautiously optimistic view about the teens she became involved with. But the teens she writes about—and, for that matter, children of ever younger ages, it seems—were allowed to withdraw into their own worlds, to disengage from their parents. That privacy won't typically end up in a Columbine-type shooting spree, though clearly the boys involved in that horror had way too much privacy. But it can result, even if just for a time, in unhealthy detachment for our kids.

I learned this lesson from my own experience (which also—for me—speaks to the folly of teens and serious dating relationships). At the tender age of fourteen, I experienced my first real love. The relationship was unbelievably intense, and it lasted for years. At the time, the sheer power of it was overwhelming—and frightening. That relationship, with its passion and jealousy and intensity, was truly dangerous. It couldn't have survived in the real world, and it shouldn't have survived in my teenage world. But I lived in a rather private world, and even though my parents, who were wonderful, knew we were dating, they had no idea how intense the relationship was, because I went to great lengths to keep that from them. And so, as it is for so many teens today, my private world was a danger to me then. I kept thoughts, and feelings and hurts and pain and profound emotions, even happiness, secreted away from my parents, when, I realize now, they could have helped me sort through those things far more successfully than I did on my own.

Too much privacy is also reflected in the *Washington Post* story I mentioned in chapter 1, about middle-schoolers in an affluent northern Virginia suburb who regularly held sex parties where oral sex was the mainstay. Hello, Mom and Dad: phone home! Where were the parents? Probably trying to give their kid a little distance, a little privacy.

We have this strange view today that parents and kids, particularly teens, are natural adversaries. I don't think it has to be this way. Kids need to establish their own personhood. Parents, I think, have to relax in areas where their kids are trying to establish their own identities, and they need to give them room to do so, as long as the kids are not endangering their own hearts. But I think parents have to stay engaged with their kids—and teach their kids that they have a responsibility to remain engaged with their parents.

Here's what I mean. I have a friend who didn't allow her children's bedroom doors to be shut unless the children were dressing. When friends were visiting from school, they were welcome to go into the children's rooms, but the doors remained open. My friend didn't make a habit of listening outside the room, but her children knew that their lives were open to their parents.

Similarly, my friend allowed her children to have passwords on computers, but she always had access to them. That doesn't mean that she constantly looked into what her children were up to, only that her children understood that she, and their dad, had a right—and sometimes even a responsibility—to do so. These rules created more, not less, openness in that family. Now that the children are grown, it's fair to say that it served them well.

Many successful parents have worked to establish an early pattern of open communication that simply becomes habit. For instance, in the grade-school years, parents might ask, "Who did you sit next to at lunch today?" "What did you talk about?" "Who did you play with at recess today?" The child will become used to answering such questions, to having his life be an open book. Will this carry over into the more tumultuous teen years? Not entirely. But parents who establish this pattern early are persevering in trying to reach their children's hearts.

Though the parenting culture puts a high value on our children's right to privacy, it seems to me that we would be wise, as parents, to replace that with a presumption, at least, of more openness.

Schools and the Culture Wars

Many parents are terrified of public schools and what they perceive as public education's attack on more traditional cultural values. Such parents sometimes believe that parents who send their children to their neighborhood school—as opposed to a private or parochial school or home schooling—are making a big mistake. I understand their concern, but I'm not sure they are right. Here again I think we need to appropriately engage, and help our kids to think rightly about the culture.

Some public schools may present so many challenges that it would be a wise decision for some parents to choose an alternative. Other parents want a religious or home-based school for a variety of personal, family, or spiritual reasons. And that's a decision they should have the right to make.

At the same time, at the risk of sounding like one of those parents who say their kids go to the only good public school in America, our public school in Virginia was, I thought, amazing. The fourth-grade history curriculum was excellent. My child actually learned about the Declaration of Independence and the Constitution, who wrote which, and why. (Maybe that doesn't sound like much, but how many American fourth-graders can make such distinctions?) They learned about key Revolutionary and Civil War battles, and people like George Washington and Thomas Jefferson were presented as heroes, not as corrupted or flawed figures. On the other hand, the second-grade environmental curriculum was little but propaganda. And the Family Life Education curriculum ("sex ed") was way too explicit—assuming such things should be offered in the public schools at all.

So I embraced the history, helped my children to understand where the environmental material was too extreme, and opted them out of the

Family Life Education program. But I did it, I hope, with an attitude of respect for the school and the teachers. Through it all, my kids learned something about thinking for themselves, or at least thinking with discernment rather than believing everything they heard. (When I moved the kids to our Chicago suburb, I found I was incredibly fortunate— how many parents are lucky enough to get their kids into the only *two* great public school systems in America?)

Many parents want, desperately and understandably, to have as much control over the schooling environment as possible. They want to approve of every aspect of it, and I can see why. But I think it can be helpful to our kids, within certain parameters, to learn to handle classes, teachers, other students, homework projects, subject material or lack of subject material, all kinds of things that they *don't* like. Remember: the world does not, mercifully, revolve around our kids or us. They and we might do things differently if we were in control, but they're not in control and neither are we—and that's exactly how the real world is. Giving our children an appropriate taste of that, and helping them to engage positively with that reality, can be a great gift to them.

I actually think the biggest question about a school is not so much what it teaches or doesn't teach, but who our children's peers are, an issue that becomes more important as they get older. Are these the kids we want our children hanging around? What kind of influence do they have? How do they dress? What kind of values do the parents share? I've heard of some pretty racy Christian schools and some pretty staid public schools.

My kids have been homeschooled, attended private school, and are now in public school. I may or may not consider one of those other options again—I take it year by year.

To make a decision about schooling, it seems to me parents have to ask themselves if they are intimidated by the school or if they are comfortable respectfully challenging authority when it's appropriate, even if the school doesn't always respond to their satisfaction. Would it be possible for their child to thrive there in ways that particular child needs? Or is there some reason that can't happen? Most of all, are the parents comfortable allowing their children into an environment that doesn't always share their values, perhaps seeing the potentially positive aspect of helping their children to reflectively think about those different values—and deal with the reality of a world that's not in sync with their own values?

Whatever the decision, it's the parents' to make. They can't let themselves be intimidated—either into home or private schooling, or away from those options. (I know folks who are horrified that my kids attend public schools.) The issue is, what is best for your child? Do you have the confidence to persevere with your child—and against the culture if need be—whatever your decision?

The New Family

This topic hits close to home—and when it comes to the culture wars, it looms large. My own experience doesn't change what I know to be true; in fact, it only reinforces it. Divorce is a terrible thing, and it hurts children. And in every divorce, one or both parents broke a promise.

There are millions of divorced families and tens of millions of children who live in them. But we don't have to teach our children that divorce is okay just because we've become a "divorce culture." We can rise above the culture, and teach our kids that divorce is an ugly thing.

The innocent victims of divorce—particularly the children—need special care and concern. In the Bible, God says he cares especially for widows and orphans. I believe that when one spouse has left a marriage, the spouse who's left behind becomes a kind of widow (or widower) and the children become orphans who merit God's special care and the special care of the community.

Though it sounds simplistic, it is simply true that the reason divorce is so common is because too many people don't honor the commitment of marriage. There is no longer any social stigma for those who break their vows. But, what's the point of making those vows in the first place, if you can just walk away from them when they're not easy to keep? Let's face it—there are times in all of our lives when we're not exactly "wantable." If keeping our spouse relies on him or her always wanting us, that's scary. Being free to be ourselves, even being free to fail, and knowing that our spouse is committed to us anyway, is the glory of a faithful marriage. When that faithfulness is lost, the very glue of the marriage comes unstuck. And then everything and anything becomes an excuse to leave.

I don't think we have to teach our children that "families come in all shapes and sizes" and that any shape and size is as good as any other. It may be the case that some single-parent families are healthier and happier than some two-parent families. But there is no question that, generally speaking, the best place for children to grow up is in a home with their married, biological, or adoptive parents. We can twist things around as much as we like to rationalize our own ends, but that much remains true. As a single parent, I have as much desire to rationalize myself out of that truth as anyone. But I can't. Because if I did, I'd be doing a disservice to my kids.

Judith Wallerstein, Julia Lewis, and Sandra Blakeslee are the authors of the best-selling book *The Unexpected Legacy of Divorce: The 25 Year Landmark Study*. They chronicled the difficulties that face children of divorce, even into their own adulthoods.

No one, not even the single parents among us, would say, "I hope so much that my daughter grows up to be a single mom someday" or,

"I hope my son grows up to meet a great gal and eventually get divorced." Of course not—we want what's best for our kids and for our grandkids: stable, happy marriages that last a lifetime.

But sometimes, against our will, that just doesn't happen.

The children of divorce are at greater risk of emotional and social problems than their peers in two-parent homes. But this does not mean those obstacles cannot be overcome. In fact, measuring and contending with those risks head-on, not minimizing them, is one of the best ways to help our kids beat them. In any event, we single parents don't have to give up just because our job is harder, or because it might look different than that of our peers in married families. Every one of our homes is, in that sense, unique anyway. Just like our married friends, we have to persevere—however we decide that's going to look in our own home.

In many ways, all of our children—even those in two-parent homes—are at risk of devaluing marriage because of our divorce culture. As I said in the introduction, my divorce not only affects my kids, but, for instance, the kids down the street as they see another family headed by a single mom. The more they see that, the more it becomes normal to them. That's a tragedy, and so I feel a burden for those kids, too.

I want to help those kids down the street, not just my own, to think rightly about divorce. And so I think those of us who are committed to the sanctity of marriage, whether or not we ourselves are married, *must* teach whatever children we reach that people who enter into marriage are called to be committed to the marriage and to honoring their promises, for better or for worse, for richer or for poorer. And yet, we also need to be compassionate, and teach compassion, for those cases in which that has not happened.

For those of us who are heads of single-parent families, for those of us who are the victims of divorce, we can learn to speak respectfully about our former spouse, even with genuine concern about the path he or she chose. Yet we shouldn't be afraid to say, even to our own children, that sadly, the offending spouse broke a promise and was wrong to do it. In fact, if we don't communicate that truth, however gently, we deny our children a firm foundation, a solid context, for making some sense of what has happened to their world. And we're not only not standing up for our own marriage—we're not standing up for any marriage. Sadly, such views are not in vogue in either the parenting or the popular culture.

Hate the Sin, but . . .

Such thinking is hard for many people to grasp, precisely because our culture hasn't grasped the lesson of hating the sin but having compassion for the sinner. Yet when it comes to the culture wars, this may be one of the best things we can teach our kids.

It seems today that most selfish, self-destructive, greedy, unwholesome, or self-centered behavior is labeled as some kind of personality disorder, addiction, or illness. I'm not saying these things don't exist, but it appears that in our modern culture there's a clinical explanation for everything, from serial adultery to pathological lying. Apparently we also prefer to "separate the deed from the doer" when it comes to adults.

That may be because we no longer want to talk about the "s" word—sin. We seem to have lost the ability to have true compassion, true sorrow, for those caught up in sin, without excusing in any way what they are doing. Maybe that's because such compassion can only come from understanding the power of sin, especially its power in our own lives. Such an understanding can be profoundly important to our children and to our success in persevering in our rescue mission for their hearts.

By compassion for those caught up in a serious sin, I don't mean cheap forgiveness if it isn't sought. I don't mean calling the sin by some other name. I mean seeing the sin for what it is and having a sense of real sorrow for the destruction a person has caused himself, and a willingness to help him if we are in a position to do so.

I think this is different from "hate the sin, love the sinner." Too often, when we hear that expression today, there is a sense of separating the sin from the sinner. But, the sin is the expression of the heart and soul of the sinner. To separate the two is not only impossible, it would utterly rob us of our humanity. Such a view limits our agency as human actors.

When we hear about someone behaving in ways that genuinely cause hurt in her own life or those of others, there are a few typical responses. "She couldn't help it," "She's just not thinking straight," or "We have no right to judge" are common. On the other hand, when the behavior touches us personally, there may be all-out fury, or even glee at the fallen one's failure.

Whether it's a national figure who betrays a personal or financial trust or a friend who leaves her family, I think what's often lacking is the ability to have true sorrow for the person who has, perhaps, allowed sin to become all-consuming or blinding, and yet to see the sin for exactly what it is—and perhaps most important, to accept the fact that it came straight from the sinner's own heart. We may, in fact, need to make a value judgment about the sin, something our culture is loath to do. (Unless, of course, it's about smoking!)

It may be perfectly appropriate to have a sense of anger or to be indignant or hurt when someone has wronged us. And yet, how much better to have a true sense of sorrow for the one caught up in the sin, as well as the desire to genuinely do good to the person if we can. That, in fact, is the right way to love the sinner, and the way we ourselves want to be loved as sinners: in truth and in action.

An understanding of these principles can, for starters, protect us against the terrible sin of pride. Sin lives in the heart of each of us, and it's only by God's grace that some of us don't become quite as mired in it as others.

We may think that feeling righteous anger is a throwback to a judgmental past and that refusing to make value judgments is "enlightened." But really, such a view just deadens our own souls to the power of sin and keeps us from extending true compassion to the people who need it most, in a way that can help them most—by understanding that their struggle is not with some pathology but with sin itself.

Changing the name of "sin" to "personality disorder" or "illness" or "addiction" doesn't take away its power. Though I certainly agree that those factors are sometimes at play, routinely dismissing sin as something less than what it is just makes us less able to confront and fight it in our own lives and to help the people we care about fight it in theirs. Helping our children to see this truth is to give them a gift indeed.

The Culture and the Heart

We can't keep the world out of our homes, even if we turn off the TV, don't watch movies, make our girls dress in long skirts, and home-school our kids. Those might all be good things, but they will not keep sin out of the heart. And if they lead to false complacency or, worse, self-righteousness, they will be destructive influences for our kids.

Our children's biggest challenge is not the world or the culture itself, it's their own hearts. If we can teach our children to make responsible value judgments about the world they live in, to have compassion, when appropriate, for others caught up in sin, and most of all to contend with the wayward tendencies of their own hearts, we will have gone a long way toward advancing our rescue mission in our children's lives.

Sometimes, advancing that mission—teaching our children to engage (or sometimes not to engage) with the culture—puts us parents right in the middle of the culture wars.

I have a friend whose daughter was barely a teenager when she was invited to an end-of-the-year party at a school friend's house. All seemed fine, until my friend called the host child's mother. My friend wanted to know if she could provide some food or soda. As she probed a bit to find out the details of the party, she learned that there would not be a gang of children, only ten kids: five boys and five girls. Hmmm. And where would the host-mother be during the soiree? Well, not at the party. But not to worry—her fifteen-year-old son would look after the youngsters.

My friend, rightly I think, said "No way." Such a situation could put too much pressure on a young girl. (Yes, there *are* times when it's best to avoid the world, rather than engage it. Making those distinctions is one of our jobs as parents.) My friend politely let the host-mother know that her child would not be able to attend. And what was the response of my friend's child to the change of plans? Total relief. She had sensed that she might be getting in over her head and was glad to have the excuse that her mother wouldn't let her attend the party. We forget sometimes that we can protect our children by letting them use us for protection.

Other times our kids will be furious when we say no and other parents say yes. Sometimes—let's admit it—we don't want the other parents to think we're a little bit strange for not going along with the pack: parents suffer from peer pressure, too. (So just imagine how powerfully it operates on our kids.) But that's all part of engaging with the culture. Anyway, we all survived, as kids, hearing things like, "Well, I'm not Sheila's mother, I'm your mother, and the answer is still no."

In fact, I've sometimes been the mother to whom the other moms have to say no, and I respect it. For instance, my children are allowed to watch certain R-rated movies with me, if I think they're worthy and if sexual content is not an issue. The *Matrix* trilogy is a good example.

Those were phenomenally well-done and thoughtful films, even with the violence. (We did have to fast forward through one sexual scene in the second movie.)

Peter in particular enjoyed delving into the films and having discussions with others who appreciated them. On the other hand, I hated the first *Shrek* movie. Although it was rated PG, I thought it was cynical and full of gratuitous sexual references. Anyway, if I'm taking kids to a movie or putting one on in my home, I check with the other moms. Often they say, "Only G or PG movies," and I honor that. Similarly, one mom told me that she didn't want her son playing with toy cap guns at my house, although toy guns with no realistic noises were fine with her. Got it.

On the other hand, when a neighborhood couple were getting divorced (long before I did) the mom, whom I like very much, asked me to tell my kids that it was "okay" and "the right thing to do and everyone is fine with it." Well, I didn't. I told my kids that we cared about this family, we needed to take extra care of their kids now, but without knowing any of the details we knew that one or both partners in the marriage had broken a promise, and it wasn't "okay."

As parents, we have to be willing to help our kids engage rightly with the culture, and as parents we also have to engage rightly with it, or to stand up to it, ourselves.

Parenting Check

It's so much easier to think that sin is out there, in the world, and not in our child's heart. It's so much less trouble to address the former! It gives us so much security. Because then, if we just keep the world out, we're fine, right?

Can you see how we can go to great lengths to shut the world out of our children's lives, but not have protected them at all against corruption of the heart?

It's also easier to try to mold our children to our own way of thinking, rather than helping them to think rightly about *the way* they come to think about their world and make value judgments. After all, that means they might eventually have views of the world different than ours.

It can be a little scary to realize that our kids might not come to hold just the same tastes or values that we do. But the wonderful truth is that helping our children to reflect properly on their hearts, their relationships, their desires, and their world is one of the best ways we have of protecting them against the world. And one of the best tools we have for not being fearful when they don't adopt all of our views of the world.

12 To Spank or Not to Spank (and Why It's Not Really the Right Question, Anyway)

Ninety-four percent of American three- and four-year-olds were spanked by a parent in the previous year, according to a 1999 study by respected antispanking advocate Murray A. Straus. Sixty-five percent of all Americans approve of parents spanking their children, which is not much lower than the 74 percent who approved of it in 1946, according to *U.S. News & World Report*.

And yet, spanking remains the most provocative topic in all of the parenting culture, although there's actually little debate about it in those circles. That's because the experts have decided that all spanking of young children by their parents—no matter how controlled, restrained, or rare, or what the reason for it—is unacceptable.

Why the Beef?

All spanking is, by definition, child abuse, says Dr. Irwin Hyman, author of the *The Case Against Spanking*. He advocates a federal law banning parents from spanking their children. To advance his cause, he tells us that Adolf Hitler was raised by a dictatorial father: "When Hitler grew up, he learned from his family how to be a dictator. Unfortunately, he inflicted his cruelty on the world." (My guess is that General Dwight Eisenhower was spanked as a child, too.)

At a 1996 American Academy of Pediatrics conference in Elk Grove Village, Illinois, on spanking, Hyman claimed that fifty years of research has consistently shown that *all* punishment is detrimental to children. He was not able to back up that assertion. And yet he is one of America's leading antispanking advocates.

There's more: "Society as a whole, not just children, could benefit from ending the system of violent child-rearing that goes under the euphemism of spanking," the *New York Times* quotes Dr. Straus as saying.

"Parents justify, 'We don't hit our kids, we spank them.' What's the difference?" asks Dr. William Sears. Well, for starters, I would argue that if spanking is hitting, then time-outs are incarceration and removing privileges from a child is stealing.

Getting a spanking might just compel a child to learn to "charm his way out of mischief," or help a child feel absolved from a crime and so be ready to misbehave again, fears Marguerite Kelly, a dear grandmother and author of the colorful *Marguerite Kelly's Family Almanac*. That's quite an indictment based on . . . what? She doesn't tell us. And anyway, the same indictment could be true for *any* discipline if it's misused.

Where's the Beef?

Why the hysteria—I mean, referring to *Hitler*? After all, the real issue is not spanking at all. The real issue is the context of parenting within which spanking, or any discipline, is carried out. (Because that context matters so much, I oppose spanking except by parents.) I think more than anything, the furor over spanking says a great deal about today's parenting culture and raises the question of whether the parenting culture has served either parents or children well.

The number-one argument against parental spanking of children is, "If I have the right to spank my child, that teaches him that he has the right to hit others." But with that logic, confining a child in a time-out teaches him that he has the right to confine others, taking a privilege away from him teaches him that he has the right to steal from others, and so on.

A variation on this theme is, we don't hit other adults, so how can we allow the spanking of children? But this argument dissolves, too. If I make my children take a bath, do their math problems, or practice the piano, it's good parenting. If I make my postman take a bath, do math problems, or practice the piano, it would be really weird—and illegal. To question our authority in our children's lives by pointing out our lack of authority in other people's lives misses the point.

Another argument against spanking is that it's always wrong to inflict physical pain on a child. Yet we don't hesitate to do so in other instances where it's for their good. Think about how many times we hold our toddlers tight in a doctor's office while they are pierced with a needle. That hurts mom and child! Yet they will receive some twenty (painful) vaccinations in the first years of life. And no one suggests that it dooms the little one to a life of violence.

I don't think many people would say that today's children are happier, less depressed, less violent, or better behaved than those of previous generations, who were routinely spanked. But that is the implicit promise of the antispanking advocates. I'm sure they would argue that rates of spanking haven't dropped enough to yield that result. On the other hand, I am not suggesting that a lack of spankings is the primary reason we're seeing the growth of all sorts of unwholesome pathologies in kids.

That's because spanking is not the issue; the context of the parenting is.

I certainly agree that parents who are morally opposed to spanking should not do it. And I can understand parents who say, "We don't spank, but I respect the choice of other parents who do." But the antispanking advocates seem to have no such tolerance. Could it be that many advocates simply do not trust parents to do what is best for their children? Now that hurts.

The Power of Touch

We hug and kiss our little ones; we hold them and cuddle them and tell them how much we love them. Those wonderful times are little pieces of heaven on earth. Could you say "I love you with all my heart," but never kiss, hug, or cuddle your child? Would he believe you? I don't think so.

So, too, touch can be extremely important when it comes to discipline. Understanding "no" and right and wrong and "You must not" and "You must" is crucially important to the well-being of our children. Sometimes clarifying those lessons with physical touch gives them real meaning and a sense of urgency every bit as important as the touch of our love. It can be part of our rescue mission for our kids, but it's our job as parents to lovingly connect the spanking to the lesson.

I make sure my kids understand that I spank them not out of anger, or for my own satisfaction, but out of a duty to them. If they don't see that, the resentment that can well up in their hearts is understandable. But *any* discipline can produce resentment or anger in a little one if it seems to be carried out arbitrarily and not for the child's well-being.

And so when I spank my kids—it's done only on the fatty thigh, and I always tell them "one spank" or "two spanks" ahead of time to communicate to them that I am in control of myself—I make sure they know why they are being spanked, I tell them how much I love them, and when it's over I make sure all is completely forgiven and forgotten. It's the context of the parenting that counts.

Healthy Habits of the Heart

Perhaps it's hard for the antispanking advocates to see that obedience is a crucially important habit of the heart, because the habit of obedience prepares the heart for many other good and important things. If that habit is rooted early, the methods needed to reinforce the habit fall away, as the stakes of a tree are removed when it is strong enough to grow on its own.

I used to take Peter and Victoria, then about four and two years old, with me when I went to get my hair done. (We're talking cut, color, and highlights—not a short process.) I would bring crayons and coloring books and tell them to stay seated, color, and chat quietly. And they would. This always produced gasps of amazement from the hairdresser and other patrons in the shop. In turn, I was amazed: I could instruct my kids to sit down and color, and they would. *Big deal!* That was astonishing?

My children are hardly perfect—which, if you've read this far, you know. They are works in progress. But my children do understand that they are *expected* to obey, respect, and respond appropriately to me. Such things are part of the general operating principles of our home.

So many parents don't seem to expect obedience—or even simple respect—from their children. These parents sound as if such consideration is almost impossible. I'm talking about loving, conscientious parents who have no presumption that their kids will treat them with respect and honor. What is that doing to the child's heart? How can a heart that wrongly oriented be prepared to produce other good things?

When my children do behave well, I don't give spankings the credit. While antispanking advocates see spanking as wholly horrific, I don't see it as wholly anything. It's just one tool in my parental tool chest, a tool that, if it's used, must be used rightly. Even controlled, judicious spankings are only as good—or bad—as the context of the home life and all of the other efforts that are being made to reach a child's heart.

In any event, I don't have to walk around all day giving, or threatening, spankings, precisely because even when spankings are rare, and they should become more so as a child grows, they are still powerful reminders of what I expect from my children. Maybe that's why I can't remember the last time I spanked Peter, for it was years ago, and I can barely remember when I last spanked Victoria. They'll all reach that stage.

I do remember when Olivia was in the early stages of that progression. Then about eighteen months old, she was with me as I was observing Madeleine in gymnastics class. I noticed another young child, about two, cooped up in a makeshift playpen, and he was miserable. Apparently, he wouldn't obey his mom and stay in the safe "observation" area. Meanwhile, Olivia was happily walking here and there. Every once in a while, she would get near the gymnastics floor, and I would call out, "No, Olivia." She would promptly turn back.

She had begun to experience a physical no on the back of her hand at home, so simply the word "no" meant something to her. In this case she wasn't being disobedient, but she was being protected. The parenting culture might be shocked at my actions—but who had more freedom that particular morning, my child, who had experienced the physical touch of no, or that sad child in the pen who almost certainly had not?

In very young children, a spank or a swat on the hand is often not punishment, it's training, learning, communicating—and it actually sets the stage for easier and more positive training, learning, and communicating in the years ahead. As they get older, the habits of responding in a positive, respectful way should become ingrained, hopefully in the heart itself, and so the "support structure" of spanking can naturally fall away.

How Do the Alternatives Stack Up?

I respect thoughtful parents and their discipline choices for their kids. Today several disciplinary techniques besides spanking are in common use, and they're worth assessing. Whatever we use, we have to ask ourselves, does this discipline reach the heart of the child or just manipulate her behavior?

For starters, we often hear about things like removing privileges, often the same thing as so-called logical consequences, and time-outs.

Unfortunately, I've seen parents take away privileges in what I think is a total misunderstanding of what discipline should look like. For some kids, misbehaving when a friend is over today means the friend doesn't come back next week. But how is the little one supposed to connect those two things in any positive way? Further, having a friend over is a good and wholesome thing. The best way to teach our children to play well with others is to have others in the home.

"If you don't get to the dinner table on time, you won't be allowed to eat again until tomorrow morning," one parenting newsletter suggested as discipline for tardiness. But our kids need to eat. Besides, what if the child thinks, Great! We're having fish tonight, and I hate fish! And, most important, what does this discipline technique teach the child about respect for his family, obeying his parents, and arriving on time for dinner? Nothing.

There is little logic in such practices. If parents discipline their child with consequences that include taking away a good thing that is totally unrelated to the infraction, the child may learn to manipulate the system to avoid having good things taken away. In contrast, if parents instead discipline their child by enforcing "no" with real meaning, and a physical pang when necessary, the child has a chance to learn that disobedience is painful. If it is interpreted to him rightly by his parents, a child may learn that disobedience is painful most of all to his heart.

I have a dear friend who, as a boy, borrowed his father's tools but then was careless, when he knew much better, and left them out in the rain. They began to rust. A modern father might take the tools away from the child for a period of time. But, then how could the child learn to use and respect the tools rightly? But this dad gave his son a spanking, and handed the tools right back. All was forgiven. The boy was *trusted* to use and care for the tools again—correctly—which he did from then on. What a lesson that boy learned. And that sting may have saved him from a much greater pain when the stakes for carelessness would be much higher than a rusted set of tools.

Then there are "time-outs." But no one has ever successfully answered the question "What do I do when my toddler doesn't want to stay in time-out?" Recently, the website theparentcenter.com ran a long column on that very question. The answer was that the parent should keep calmly returning the child to his time-out seat. Guess who is going to win *that* game?

Maybe one spanking is worth a thousand time-outs? (Actually, spanking or the threat of a spanking has been shown to be very effective in enforcing milder disciplines, like time-outs, as I'll discuss later in the chapter.)

When I think of putting one of my children at age two or three into a time-out, it just seems sort of, well, silly. Just what, exactly, are kids supposed to learn from this? Say my daughter throws a tantrum when I put her into the car, so I put her in time-out. Then, for throwing a fit because she doesn't want to go in the car, her punishment is . . . being taken out of the car? Doesn't really seem to make the point. (For the record, I do think removing a child from a situation where he's just too wound up or there's too much excitement can be fine, but that's not discipline.)

Dr. Perri Klass, a pediatrician, wrote a very funny column for *Parenting* magazine. She admitted that while she offers advice to new parents all the time, in her own life she finds herself yelling at her kids a lot. I thought this was pretty candid. For the record, I'm good at "Stop it, now!" really, really loud, *and* I can pound a tabletop at the same time. Dr. Klass admits that she's never succeeded in putting one of her children in time-out.

Then there's the popularly advised practice of ignoring bad behavior. Certainly there are times when it makes sense to ignore a child's irritating habits and even to pick our behavior battles. But, if we consistently ignore what we *know* to be bad behavior, on some level we are condoning it—and in any event ignoring it doesn't reach the heart.

I think whatever discipline parents use, they should genuinely ask themselves, is this discipline reaching the child's heart—or teaching her to manipulate the system? If parents can honestly say it's reaching the heart, then that is success. I believe that success is more easily achieved and discipline can be used far more sparingly when judicious spankings are at least one tool in parents' discipline tool chest.

Ideas from Left Field

In contrast, some of the antispanking advocates' ideas for handling tricky situations are pretty wacky. Irwin Hyman, for instance, says he's concerned about any physical force parents might use. But, he readily admits, when kids are out of control or physically attacking someone, "Parents have the right and responsibility to assert themselves in such situations and to use force when necessary to protect themselves, others or property, or to prevent children from self-injury." Right. (Apparently, parents sometimes have the responsibility to use their physical advantage after all.) Hyman advises physical restraint as one option for de-escalating an incident: "The 'hold' requires grasping children from behind by their wrists, forearms, or upper arms in a manner that their arms are crossed and locked," he writes. "This technique allows you, assuming you are strong enough, to physically restrain and control children and prevents them from hurting themselves, or you. There are also methods of take-downs and release that you can use when the child grabs you."

Hyman may hope to argue that this is a last resort. Still, if we're going along with the advocates' overall argument against physical punishment, doesn't this method teach the child that he has the right to use take-downs and releases on others? Hyman says after a few months these kinds of practices produce results. A few *months*? Why put the child and parents through all this? It sounds like something out of professional wrestling.

This is the same man who advocates a federal law against spanking because it's "abusive."

Come, Let Us Reason Together

What about reasoning? Well, that's *it*. Reasoning with our kids is exactly where we hope to get with successful discipline. It means thinking through the misbehavior, why it's serious, how it affected others, helping our children understand how it affected their hearts. Reasoning is crucial to getting to the heart of the child. In the Bible, in Isaiah 1:18, God says, "Come now . . . let us reason together, though your sins were as scarlet they should be as white as snow." That's the model we want for our relationship with our kids.

The entire point of our actions is to help shape our child's heart so that it responds to wisdom and rejects foolishness, so that it's a heart that is in the habit of obedience, and honoring Mom and Dad. The reinforcement of physical discipline, which may be necessary at first to support and strengthen growth of the heart, is eventually gone and what remains is a heart that is, we can hope, willing, even eager, to listen to reason.

What does the research say about all this? Maybe not what you've been led to believe. But one thing *is* clear: spanking is not the issue—parenting is.

Spanking Studies Gone Wild

Murray A. Straus's 1994 book *Beating the Devil Out of Them* got rave reviews from the parenting culture for his conclusion that spanking children "leads to many social and psychological problems. These problems range from attacks on siblings to juvenile delinquency, wife beating, depression, disturbed sexual behavior, to lower occupational success and income." (I sometimes can't help wondering how the American republic has survived up to now.)

In 1997, Straus had published the results of another study in the *Archives of Pediatrics and Adolescent Medicine.* The American Medical Association, which publishes the journal, reported the findings in a press release: "Spanking makes children violent, antisocial," and it was similarly reported in scores of other news items.

But referring to these studies, *U.S. News & World Report* said in an in-depth article on spanking that "the problem with Straus and Hyman's pronouncements was that they were based on a body of research that is at best inconclusive and at worst badly flawed."

U.S. News noted that the 1997 findings were reported by the three major broadcast networks and more than one hundred newspapers and magazines, but "neither the press release nor many of the news reports mentioned the study's gaps." Those gaps included the fact that Straus studied only six- to nine-year-olds who were spanked several times a week, which is probably not representative of typical families and may indicate a poor parenting context overall. As *U.S. News* pointed out, these kids may "have severe behavioral problems quite apart from being spanked." In addition, "the 807 mothers in the survey were just 14 to 24 years old at the time [their children were born] . . . hardly a representative sample."

But the study on spanking that has gotten by far the most public attention in recent years was published in 2002 by Elizabeth Gershoff, a psychologist and researcher at Columbia University's National Center for Children in Poverty in New York City, in the *Psychological Bulletin.* Gershoff's was not a new study, but instead a review of six decades of research on corporal punishment. She found, according to the Associated Press, that "parents who spank their children risk long-term harm that outweighs the short-term benefit of instant obedience." Gershoff concluded that spanking was beneficial only in producing "immediate compliance."

Good Morning America headlined its broadcast on the study this way: "60 Years of Research Shows Spanking Children Can Cause More

Problems Than It Solves." This was right in line with almost every other press report on Gershoff's findings. But in her study, Gershoff herself in no way claimed that spankings caused these outcomes.

Gershoff herself notes the fact that she found no causal relationship between spanking and the negative outcomes she measured, only correlations. To illustrate the difference: there is an extremely high correlation between people who are in hospitals and people who are sick. But does that mean hospitals *cause* people to be sick?

But Gershoff doesn't acknowledge the biggest shortcoming in her meta-analysis: a significant number of the studies she reviewed had, to some extent, definitions of spanking that most people would deem too severe if not abusive. Drs. Diana Baumrind, Robert Larzelere, and Philip Cowan pointed this out in a response to Gershoff's study, also published in the *Psychological Bulletin* in 2002. They noted that while her analysis did exclude studies of physical punishment that she said would "knowingly" cause severe injury to a child, there are many ways to physically punish a child that might not knowingly cause "severe injury," but that are still quite harsh or abusive.

Here are examples of what two-thirds of the studies Gershoff examined for her findings on spankings and aggressiveness/antisocial behavior included as part of their descriptions of corporal punishment: "slapped on face, head and ears," "shook," "throwing something at the child," and "hit with belt, stick." That's a good way to get skewed results in the "most comprehensive study ever done on spanking."

Just as the very same medicine in the right dosage can save a patient but in the wrong dosage can be fatal, just as we need food to live but too much can make us sick or even kill us, it's extremely important to separate out judicious spanking not just from abuse but also from overly severe and even abusive use of spanking.

In addition, many of the studies Gershoff looked at focused on spanking in older children, even children well into their teens, rather than young children, where spanking is most commonly used. Also, when it came to aggressiveness and kids who were spanked, Gershoff could not answer the all-important question: Were they spanked more because they were more aggressive to begin with?

Finally, Gershoff relied on recall studies in her review of the effects of corporal punishment on adult aggression, criminality, mental health, and physical abuse. Even Gershoff admits it's easy for people to blame their current depression or other problems on corporal punishment doled out decades ago by Mom and Dad.

Gershoff herself in her study says, Look, 90 percent of adults were spanked as kids, but most have not become violent criminals, which "contradicts an assertion that corporal punishment necessarily has negative effects on children."

But perhaps most fascinating, Gershoff allows that when corporal punishment is planned, controlled, intended for the child's good, and not accompanied by strong parental emotion (exactly how it should be done, I say), it is considered "instrumental." She adds: "Children who believe that their parents are acting in their best interests, who see the discipline as appropriate to the misdeed, or who see their parents' use of force as legitimate will be inclined to accept their parents' message."

That didn't make it into the press reports of the study either.

Is it possible, then, that the advocates' attempts to undermine the legitimacy of spanking are causing parents to feel more guilty, less confident, and more furtive about spanking? Might this mean that more children are being spanked impulsively and in anger, in a way that is actually more harmful to little ones? Now, *that's* a question I'd like to see answered.

When I talked to Gershoff, she was very straightforward about the limitations of her study and readily admitted that the press did not pick up on some of the caveats she herself noted. Still, Gershoff used the language of breathless advocacy to describe her study when she wrote, "Americans need to reevaluate why we believe it is reasonable to hit young, vulnerable children, when it is against the law to hit other adults, prisoners and even animals."

It's not surprising that many of the people writing the network and newspaper stories reported the study as having virtually closed the case on spanking. They wanted big headlines, and they bought right into the thinking of the parenting culture. And they didn't read the study.

Case Open on Spanking

It seems "case open" is more appropriate. What would the science be like if we could get more clarity on whether or not there was a *causal* relationship between spanking and positive or negative outcomes for kids? Dr. Robert Larzelere attempted to answer this question in a peer-reviewed study that appeared in 2000 in *Clinical Child and Family Psychology Review.*

Dr. Larzelere, a professor at the University of Nebraska Medical Center, has been doing research on parental discipline for more than twenty years. (He presented an earlier review of spanking studies at the 1996 American Academy of Pediatrics conference on spanking where Drs. Straus and Hyman also made presentations, and here's what happened: the two conference organizers, pediatricians who originally opposed spanking, wrote later in the journal *Pediatrics,* as reported in *U.S. News & World Report,* that they had changed their minds—and came to think that maybe in loving parental hands, spanking could be okay.)

Larzelere does not urge parents to spank their children. However, he says that the evidence shows that spanking can be effective when used appropriately by parents, particularly when it is used to back up milder forms of discipline such as time-outs.

Again, it's parenting, not spanking, that is the issue.

Here's how Larzelere drew his conclusions for his 2000 review: he looked at all available studies on spanking done between 1979 and 2000, with some selected studies going back to 1938. To be included, the studies generally had to be in peer-reviewed professional journals in English. They had to include original data. The study could not be dominated by severity or abusiveness; the average age of the child when spanked had to be younger than thirteen years; and the spankings had to clearly precede the outcome measured.

These criteria produced a grand total of thirty-eight studies (sixteen of which were also included in the Gershoff review). Of those thirty-eight, seventeen studies took into account the initial level of child misbehavior, a necessity in resolving the question of whether the child was being spanked because he misbehaved or vice versa, a question that plagues spanking studies. (No wonder Larzelere says we need a lot more science here.)

What Larzelere found is that the outcomes for spanking changed dramatically depending on the research design. The four most rigorous studies, those which essentially used the same criteria the FDA requires for drug approval, found that spanking was effective in making persistently defiant two- to six-year-olds cooperate with time-out so that their parents could regain control of their behavior. Perhaps more important, related studies show that reducing this defiance to normal age levels was, in turn, essential for reducing fighting and regaining parental affection for these more difficult children. (So, maybe spanking can help a parent's heart, too!)

In these studies, then, the implied threat of a spanking, or a spanking itself, typically caused other discipline measures perhaps preferred by the parents to become more effective, sometimes far more effective, than they would otherwise be.

Throughout his study, Larzelere found that the more specific and observational the study, the more the studies took into account the initial behavior of the child, and the more they ruled out overly severe physical punishment, the more the studies showed positive outcomes when it came to parental spanking of young children.

Larzelere also points out this little nugget buried deep in a 1998 Straus study published in *Behavioral Sciences and the Law*: Straus found that alternative disciplinary methods—such as reasoning and time-outs—predicted antisocial problems in children *ten times more strongly* than did nonimpulsive physical punishment, and they predicted child impulsivity *three times more strongly*. Straus doesn't want to rule out these disciplinary techniques, but he wants to rule out spanking, which has a much weaker correlation with bad outcomes for kids.

This view tells us far more about the parenting culture than it does about the implications of spanking.

What's the Question Again?

There's a reason I've dragged you—if you've made it this far—through these various studies. It's not just to expose the zealous nature of the antispanking bias behind them, and behind the reporting on them. And it's not just to demonstrate that the antispanking advocates may, in fact, have done American children a real disservice in dissuading parents from using a legitimate and effective form of discipline.

It's to get back to the point that the real question is not whether or not to spank; it's about the whole context of the parenting. The advocates would have us believe that spanking is a primary cause of harm. Straus thinks, for instance, that lowered rates of spanking would lead to lower crime and costs for mental health treatment. If only it were that easy.

It's helpful to see that the studies showing the negative results of spanking are not at all what they seem; that other forms of discipline can also have detrimental outcomes; and that the most carefully constructed studies on spanking young children (few though they are) show it to have generally positive outcomes. Even so, it makes perfect sense to me that we should see differences in the results of studies on spanking.

That's because a decision to spank or not spank a child is not a magic pill to parental success. I've talked about why and how a loving and judicious spanking can be part of an effective rescue mission for our children. But it must be done in such a way that we, and our kids, truly understand that it is for the good of our children, not for our own satisfaction.

And isn't that true of parenting itself? The right question is not "to spank or not to spank"; it is, What is the context of my parenting as a whole?

The zealotry of the antispanking advocates may just be a metaphor for what we parents are up against in the parenting culture: The experts are nervous about the idea that we parents might know better than our kids, but, it seems, they are often convinced they know better than we parents do. The lightning rod issue of spanking—and the extent of spanking studies gone wild—is just another example of how we have to be bold and confident in our role as parents. We have to challenge the experts for the sake of our children.

Parenting Check

Nobody should bully you into spanking, or not spanking, your kids. You as the parent have to decide what's best for your children when it comes to discipline.

How do you define successful discipline? Is it just getting the right behavior at the moment, or is it reaching the heart?

It might help to think through various methods of discipline, how they are used in your home, and what your child might be learning from them. When your children are forty, what will they say about how you disciplined them? About whether it was effective and communicated love? About whether it was for your good or theirs? About whether it had a positive impact on their souls?

13 Challenge the Experts for the Sake of Your Child

A century after the beginning of the Century of the Child, it turns out that the experts haven't succeeded in re-creating children in their new and better image after all.

There was a sense, at the dawn of the twentieth century, that we really could remake children. Given the new vistas of scientific knowledge that had seemed to open up, these worthies more than one hundred years ago thought we could make children better and, if not perfect, well, darn close.

There was L. Emmett Holt, who guaranteed that his infant-care regimes could make babies and moms healthier and calmer. There was G. Stanley Hall, who claimed to have invented adolescence. John Watson told mothers they ought not hug and kiss their children but should give them a handshake in the morning instead. There was the famous Dr. Benjamin Spock, as well as Bruno Bettelheim, Arnold Gesell, and Penelope Leach. Often, these experts contradicted not only one another but also themselves. Parents heard about tough love and soft love, parent-centered parenting and child-centered parenting . . . and every expert promised better babies, smarter babies, or more attached babies and more responsible or more loving children—whatever was in vogue for children at the moment. (For more on this history see sociologist Ann Hulbert's excellent 2003 book, *Raising America: Experts, Parents, and a Century of Advice About Children.*)

But a hundred years later, we're struggling with problems that those early, optimistic child experts wouldn't have likely thought possible. They wouldn't have forecast widespread behavior problems, increasingly common extreme behavior problems, depression, addictions, sexual promiscuity, ever more "disorders" of childhood, and so on. Could anyone? And that in spite of the fact that many of those experts from the Century of the Child gave us great knowledge about the emotional and physical workings of children (while others have been wholly or partly discredited).

I'm hardly blaming such pathologies on the parenting culture. I'm just pointing out the obvious: one hundred years of expert advice on child raising hasn't changed kids for the better.

The rise of the child expert *has* had at least one demonstrable impact—it's made too many parents terrified to trust themselves when it comes to parenting their kids.

So, given the at best questionable record of a history of parenting gurus, why do so many parents continue to religiously abide by the teachings of the modern-day parenting expert? Why is the parenting culture still so powerful in the popular culture? Why is it that, if you asked most mainstream parents a few questions, they would answer right back: "Always give your child choices." "Never spank." "Build self-esteem." "Find alternatives to no." And, for heaven's sake, "Criticize the behavior, never the child."

I think we still labor under the impression that we really can have more perfect children. If only we "attachment-parent" or listen ever more carefully to our kids and their feelings or find creative ways to disguise "no"—if we just build their self-esteem properly—well, the sky's the limit on what we can accomplish. Too often, we don't see ourselves on a rescue mission; we see ourselves on a "perfecting" mission. Maybe even on a mission to be perfect parents.

And so we've come to idealize, and idolize, our children. We seem to have bought into the ridiculous idea that mothers since the beginning of time have been having three hours a day of floor-time with their littlest ones and, if they weren't, well then, they weren't very good mothers, were they? We've accepted that we can never say, "I'm busy, dear. Go play with your friends," because of what that might do to a child's tender psyche.

In contrast, letting go of perfection in our children and in ourselves would be to let go of a whole lot of fear and meet with a whole lot of enjoyment in parenting. As I said in the introduction, I think the parenting culture—and, by extension, many parents—just has to lighten up.

I'm not at all suggesting that parents turn up their collective nose at the parenting culture. In this book, I've quoted experts who I think have good things to say. I've also spent many chapters challenging many experts and their advice, really their dictates, to parents.

The only important question is, What do you as the parent think of what the experts have to say? Does it make sense? That's for you, and you alone, to decide. In the end I'm encouraging you as the parent to have confidence in what *you* think.

I am suggesting that we parents not be tyrannized by the experts. And that the first step to getting away from the tyranny of the experts is understanding that our children are not the fragile hothouse flowers we've been led to believe. They might benefit greatly from learning that they are not the center of the universe, and we parents might also benefit greatly from realizing that our children don't have to be.

Perhaps the second step is coming to see that most of us have normal, average kids. As a general rule, we're not raising the next Mother

Teresa, Mozart, Babe Ruth, or Albert Einstein. *And that's fine!* So many Americans labor under the misperception that they're raising wildly above average kids; it would be funny if it weren't so silly. Of course, we want our kids to do the best they can do, to be the best people they can be, and we want to encourage them to those ends. But deep down, is that really enough for us?

Victoria was recently tested with her peers as a way of identifying "gifted" children. (Standard procedure in our former public school.) When the test results came back, I glanced at them only briefly before filing them away. So I had to laugh when an e-mail from the teacher to all the parents in the class explained that she had been deluged by parents contacting her about whether or not their child's scores qualified them for the gifted program. They were just going to *have* to wait until September for more information about where this year's "gifted cutoff" would be.

A psychologist friend of mine who practices in New York City has told me that New York parents are all convinced that their child is in the ninety-fifth percentile of children in the city when it comes to intelligence. (You do the math.) Maybe our culture has become so achievement-oriented that it was inevitable that we would apply that standard to our kids, too.

We parents need to get comfortable with the fact that most of our children are delightfully, wonderfully, magically, uniquely average. Every one of them has strengths, and sometimes those strengths are extraordinary; every one of them has weaknesses, and those can be pretty extraordinary, too. Still, nothing qualifies them to be the center of the universe.

Maybe one of the things that leads us to be tyrannized by the experts is a reluctance to grasp the fact that it's okay for our kids to be ordinary. If our child *is* less than perfect in any way, well gosh darn it, there's got to be an expert out there who can make him better! If only we can find the magic formula to get the tantrums under control, make him more social, help him to be more charming, lead him to be smarter, well then, he'll have the world in the palm of his hand.

It's no wonder so many books and articles on parenting make all sorts of promises. Just follow this expert's advice, and voilà! The alternative is: don't follow this expert's advice and your child is doomed.

At the beginning of the twentieth century, despite the fact that Americans had been raising children with some degree of success for quite some time, we were told that what children *really* required was expert handling and instruction. That gave children a whole new status. Rather than human beings, they were turned into rather angelic science experiments—experiments that could go horribly wrong if not handled *perfectly*.

The definition of "handled perfectly" may have changed wildly, but somebody out there had the answer, if we could only find the right expert or the right scientists with the right advice. Once we believe we can create more perfect children, if our child misses that mark then something must really be wrong.

With four young kids, I'm used to being bombarded with advice from the experts on how I should be raising them. But from day one, it was amazing to me how little of it made sense. I was fortunate to have a community of wise, experienced parents who weren't on a jihad against the experts, but who would just laugh and say things like, "Of *course* you need to be in charge of your children." "Criticize the behavior and not the child? What does that do for the little one?" Often, they just gave me the confidence to trust my own instincts, to ask and answer for myself the question "What makes sense here?"

Such wise parents also helped me see that it's only confident parents who can really benefit from sound advice from the experts. Rather than eschewing it all, confident parents have the wherewithal to pick out the wisdom, shrug their shoulders at what doesn't make sense, and leave the rest of it behind. Or at least admit that it doesn't help. We can do this without feeling one bit guilty about it. The parents who don't have confidence in their own instincts are the ones who get tossed pillar to post by the latest parenting advice and remain constantly fearful that they are doing the wrong things, or not enough of the right ones.

My wise friends helped me to understand that my mission couldn't just be stopping the backtalk, ending the tantrums, or getting my kids to quit squabbling. My mission was to go much further than that. I had to understand that my children's hearts were in danger, from themselves even more than from the world, and I had to be on a rescue mission for those hearts. Understanding that, I'm in a much better position to make use of the experts' advice when it's helpful.

I like to say that my goal for my children is heaven, not Harvard. If they go to Harvard on their way to heaven, I suppose that's great. But if I'm so focused on getting them into Harvard that I don't think about the much larger goal of helping their hearts become ready for heaven, then I have failed them. What a tragedy that would be. The parenting culture does not have heaven as its goal for my children.

Parents need to understand that when it comes to our own kids, the parenting culture does not know or love them the way we do. It does not have responsibility or authority in their lives the way we do. And as we can see from a century of wildly conflicting, often absurd, and even hilarious advice, the experts certainly don't know more, at least about our own kids, than we parents do.

It's parents who *aren't* intimidated by the parenting culture who will typically be in the best position to be a help to their kids.

Consider the schools. So often I see and hear about children who are a little bit different: he prefers to play by himself at recess, she cries easily, he daydreams a bit too much. Whatever the problem, the school counselor is often called to the scene, the parents are hauled in, and a protocol is established for various therapies to handle the "problem," which might not really be a problem to begin with. But parents don't have to be intimidated by the experts nor do they have to be so fearful if they refuse to see such behaviors as a problem. Sometimes wise outsiders can spot an issue a loving parent can't clearly see, but it's up to the parent to make good use of that information.

One year, one of my young children's teachers created far more problems than she solved. She didn't think my child was being social enough, and the child occasionally welled up in tears. The teacher asked me to meet with her to develop a protocol for this child. So I met with the teacher and heard what she had to say. I was concerned, but I didn't panic, because I had seen similar behavior at home and it had passed quickly. On the other hand, I didn't ignore what the teacher told me either.

I consulted my child's other teachers to learn their observations. I didn't let myself get intimidated by the teacher or by her legitimate concerns for my child. I didn't stomp out and tell her she didn't know what she was talking about. I took in the information, considered and investigated it, and then followed a course I felt was best for that child. I might not always be right, but I am always the child's parent, and the one in all the world most committed to that child's good.

I explained to my child's teacher that this little one was not interested in being a social butterfly but was happy with a couple of good friends. I suggested that she relax a bit and not call attention to my child every time she felt the child was getting frustrated. I asked her to try let my child work it out without her interference. I asked her to keep me apprised of what was happening, and we'd see how things went for a while. The minute the teacher backed off, things began to get so much better for my little one.

Early in another child's first-grade year, the school guidance counselor visited the classroom. She explained to the kids that they could come see her if they had a problem. All they had to do was fill out a form that would be sent to her office. The form had pictures of friends, family, and schoolwork, among others, and the kids were told to circle one of the pictures to describe their problem. I knew, of course, that the school had counselors. I just didn't know they were going to encourage the kids to share problems with them one on one—problems the kids might not have even known they had.

I have no difficulty with parents seeking psychological or other intervention for their child, but I think children should be encouraged to talk to their parents first. Certainly I think that the parents should be called to see if the child has their permission to talk with a counselor. I also believe that what's said in any such meeting should be shared with the parents. This pattern reinforces the connection that children and parents are on the same team, that Mom and Dad have their child's interests at heart. (In our school, parents had to actively opt children out of one-on-one counseling—which I did.)

I think many school counselors are great, particularly when they meet with classes to discuss issues like study skills and how to handle bullies. And there may be a place for private discussions with them, as long as Mom and Dad are involved at a level at which they feel comfortable. (Cases involving suspected parental abuse are obviously different.)

But this issue involving my little one led me to write a column in which I wrote about how I told my kids, "If any adult ever says to you, 'Let's not tell your parents,' or 'Let's keep this a secret from your parents,' that person is trouble." Many school counselors do not say such things, by the way. My point was a larger one. Under ordinary circumstances, *any person* trying to come between a child and his or her parents, the people who love the child most in the world, is bad news. It doesn't matter if the person is a doctor, a teacher, or a next-door neighbor; if an adult attempts to cut Mom and Dad out of the picture with the children, that should be a red flag to our children that that adult is a problem, and our kids need to tell us about him right away. (This wariness can protect a child from far worse things than an overly meddlesome adult. For one thing, I don't think there's a child molestor since the beginning of time who hasn't told the child, "Let's keep this a secret from Mom and Dad.")

Well, I was inundated with responses from school counselors. Here's what one wrote to me:

> I take great offense at the uninformed message you chose to send to many members of the community. Additionally, it is unfortunate that you would deny your child the services and support of trained professionals to allow her the opportunity to develop her full potential and become a contributing member of society. . . . Parents and children are so closely united within their family that parents struggle to acknowledge the required learning that is necessary outside of the protected home environment. Through the development of a team approach between parents and school counselors (along with others) who have been specifically trained to address these issues in the societal context, your daughter can be exposed to valuable life lessons.

This is someone who really believes "It takes an expert to raise a child." It's almost a caricature of the parenting culture. How did children ever grow up normally before the advent of trained professionals?

It's actually confident parents, those who are persevering in their child's life, who are on a rescue mission for their child's heart, who can benefit most from listening to what others in their child's life have to say (as we parents *should* do). That's because such parents are best equipped to use that information for their child's good. So I would encourage parents everywhere to recognize the obvious: *the experts don't know it all*. We parents don't need to fear them, we don't need to be intimidated by them, nor do we need to wholly reject their advice out of a terror that it's "all or nothing" with the parenting culture.

We parents *do* need to reclaim authority in our children's lives, and to think rightly about how the experts think about raising kids.

I did not want to become a single mom, but in the process I was in some ways given the gift of having to reexamine my life, my goals, and my priorities for my children. So often we get into patterns and ways of thinking and we just get *used* to them. Sometimes it takes adversity to shake us up and help us value what really matters. I know that in the wake of my own ordeal, I came to see more clearly than ever that how we raise our children, and whether we persevere with them, really matters in terms of the kind of people they become. And so I became more purposeful than ever in pursuing my children's hearts. Though that mission looks different now, though it's more complicated, and though I'm not going to hold myself to some impossibly high standard, I am more determined in that mission than ever before.

So, I hope that what I've said in this book is helpful and that it has convinced you that you are the parent, *and that that really means something*. All I'm hoping is that while reading *It Takes a Parent* you asked yourself, Does this make sense? Do I see that I need to persevere in my rescue mission for my child's heart, whatever that particular mission looks like in my home?

I think that if we parents can reclaim the confidence to start asking that question every time we hear something else coming down the pike from the parenting culture, we have won an important victory. For you are the parent, you have a unique authority in your child's life, and you really do know better than your child. This is why you have the authority and the calling in your child's life to persevere and pursue a rescue mission for his heart. If you put the book down more convinced than ever of these truths, then I've accomplished my goal in writing it.

And if we parents begin to believe that our children typically don't really require expert handling, that they are wonderfully ordinary and much loved little people who require *our* handling, maybe that will help us get them off that dangerous pedestal, too.

I know that we parents can live up to that calling. After all, we love our kids as no one else does. We go through so much for them. We sacrifice so much for them. We think about them so much. We want to do the right thing. The unconditional love a parent has for a child is very powerful. If we parents put half the energy into thinking, "Does this really make sense?" that we put into thinking, "What do the experts say?" I'm convinced we'd turn the parenting culture inside out.

And that would be a good thing. *Not* because the parenting culture doesn't have some good ideas, but because we parents would be back in the driver's seat of deciding which of the parenting culture's ideas are good for our family and which aren't.

That would mean we parents would no longer be tyrannized by the experts. And that would greatly benefit our kids.

If you disagree with me on all sorts of issues—whether it's spanking children or the necessity of building their self-esteem—but you walk away more convinced of the basic tenets of confident parenting I've outlined, you have challenged the experts. You have dared to parent. And you have given your children an incredible gift.

Sources

Introduction

Key, Ellen, *The Century of the Child*. New York: G. P. Putnam's Sons, 1909.

Chapter 1. Kids Gone Wild

Carton, Barbara. "Need Help with a Cranky Kid? Frazzled Parents Call a Coach." *The Wall Street Journal*, May 22, 2003.

Crocker, Kellye Carter. "Are You a Parent or a Pushover?" *Parents*, January 2004, 90–93.

Easterbrook, Gregg. *The Progress Paradox*. New York: Random House, 2003.

"Final Report on the 3rd Annual National Survey of School-Based Police Officers." National Association of School Resource Officers (NASRO), Cleveland, 2003.

Shaw, Robert. *The Epidemic: The Rot of American Culture, Absentee and Permissive Parenting, and the Resultant Plague of Joyless, Selfish Children*. New York: ReganBooks, 2003.

Stepp, Laura Sessions. "Parents Are Alarmed by an Unsettling New Fad in Middle Schools: Oral Sex." *The Washington Post*, July 8, 1999, A1.

Tripp, Tedd. *Shepherding a Child's Heart*. Wapwallopen, Penn.: Shepherd Press, 1995.

Vedantam, Shankar. "FDA Links Antidepressants, Youth Suicide Risk." *The Washington Post*, February 3, 2004.

Wallis, Claudia. "Does Kindergarten Need Cops?" *Time*, December 15, 2003, 52–53.

"Youth Violence: A Report of the Surgeon General." Surgeon General of the United States, Washington, D.C., 2001.

Chapter 2. Perseverance: Mission Possible

Bridges, Lisa, and Kristin Anderson Moore. "Religious Involvement and Children's Well-Being: What Research Tells Us (and What It Doesn't)." *Child Trends Research Brief*, Washington, D.C., 2002.

Harris, Judith Rich. *The Nurture Assumption: Why Children Turn Out the Way They Do.* New York: Simon & Schuster, 1998.

Jang, Sung Joon. "Age-Varying Effect of Family, School, and Peers on Delinquency: A Multilevel Modeling Test of Interactional Theory." *Criminology*, no. 37, 1999, 643–685.

McNeely, Clea, et al. "Mothers' Influence on the Timing of First Sex Among 14- and 15-year-olds." *Journal of Adolescent Health*, vol. 31, no. 3, 2002, 256–265.

Nash, Madeleine. "The Personality Genes." *Time*, April 27, 1998, 60–61.

"National Household Survey on Drug Use and Health." Department of Health and Human Services (HHS), Substance Abuse and Mental Health Services Administration (SAMHSA), Washington, D.C., 2003.

Okagaki, Lynn, Kimberly Hammond, and Laura Seaman. "Socialization of Religious Beliefs." *Journal of Applied Developmental Psychology*, vol. 20, no. 2, 1999, 273–294.

"Study Finds Parental Influence Still Important During Adolescence." Ohio State University, August 25, 1999. Press release.

Chapter 3. I'm on Your Side
(What's a Parent for, Anyway?)

Faculty of Tufts University's Eliot-Pearson Department of Child Development. *Proactive Parenting: Guiding Your Child from Two to Six.* New York: Berkley Books, 2003.

Hymowitz, Kay. *Ready or Not: Why Treating Children as Small Adults Endangers Their Future—and Ours.* New York: The Free Press, 1999.

Sears, William. *The Successful Child: What Parents Can Do to Help Kids Turn Out Well.* Boston: Little, Brown, 2002.

Chapter 5. Our Children, Our Idols

Coles, Robert. "Growing Up in America, Then and Now." *Time*, December 29, 1975, 27–29.

Dalton, Patricia. "Let Go, Already. If It's All About the Children, the Children Will Never Leave." *The Washington Post*, December 29, 2002, B1.

Grossman, Lev. "They Just Won't Grow Up." *Time*, January 24, 2005, 42–54.

Jennings, Lisa. "Second Child Changes a Woman's Life." Scripps Howard News Service, May 7, 2001.

Mogel, Wendy. *The Blessing of a Skinned Knee*. New York: Penguin, 2002.

Chapter 6. The Self-Delusion of Self-Esteem

Baumeister, Roy, and Brad Bushman. "Threatened Egotism, Narcissism, Self-Esteem, and Direct and Displaced Aggression: Does Self-Love or Self-Hate Lead to Violence?" *Journal of Personality and Social Psychology*, no. 57, 1998, 219–229.

Briggs, Dorothy Corkille. *Your Child's Self-Esteem*. Pella, Ia.: Main Street Books, 1975.

Dweck, Carol. *Self-Theories: Their Role in Motivation, Personality and Development*. New York: Psychology Press, 1999.

Emler, Nicholas. *Self-Esteem: The Costs and Causes of Low Self-Worth*. York, England: York Publishing Services, 2001.

Goode, Erica. "Deflating Self-Esteem's Role in Society's Ills." *The New York Times*, October 1, 2002, F1.

Loomans, Diane. *Today I Am Lovable—365 Positive Activities for Kids*. Tiburon, Calif.: Starseed Press, 1996.

McKay, Matthew, and Patrick Fanning. *Self-Esteem*. New York: St. Martin's Press, 1987.

Payne, Lauren Murphy, and Claudia Rohling. *A Leader's Guide to Just Because I Am: A Child's Book of Affirmation*. Minneapolis: Free Spirit Publishing, 1994.

Chapter 7. Misbehavior and Other Matters of the Heart

Eisenberg, Arlene, Heidi Murkoff, and Sandee Hathaway. *What to Expect: The Toddler Years*. New York: Workman Publishing, 1994.

Kluger, Jeffrey. "Medicating Young Minds." *Time*, November 3, 2003, 48–58.

Mogel, Wendy. *The Blessing of a Skinned Knee*. New York: Penguin, 2002.

Welch, Edward T. *Blame It on the Brain: Distinguishing Chemical Imbalances, Brain Disorders, and Disobedience*. Phillipsburg, N.J.: P&R Publishing, 1998.

Chapter 8. When Did "No" Become a Dirty Word?

"Childhood Behavior Problems Predict Emotional Baggage for Young Adults." Pennsylvania State University, September 11, 2000. Press release.

Eisenberg, Arlene, Heidi Murkoff, and Sandee Hathaway. *What to Expect: The Toddler Years.* New York: Workman Publishing, 1994.

Faculty of Tufts University's Eliot-Pearson Department of Child Development. *Proactive Parenting: Guiding Your Child from Two to Six.* New York: Berkley Books, 2003.

Knoester, Chris. "Do Childhood Behavior Problems Predict Outcomes in Young Adulthood?" Paper presented at the American Sociological Association conference, Washington, D.C., 2000.

Lumeng, Julie. "Association Between Clinically Meaningful Behavior Problems and Overweight in Children." *Pediatrics,* vol. 112, 2003, 1138–1145.

Sears, William. *The Discipline Book: How to Have a Better Behaved Child from Birth to Age Ten.* Boston: Little, Brown, 1995.

————. "The Fewer the No's the Better Your Day Goes." Presentation at La Leche League International Conference, Chicago, 1995.

Shaw, Robert. *The Epidemic: The Rot of American Culture, Absentee and Permissive Parenting, and the Resultant Plague of Joyless, Selfish Children.* New York: ReganBooks, 2003.

Sims, Karen. "Dealing with Power Struggles." *Positive Parenting,* January 1996. Newsletter (Ventura, Calif.).

Stuart, Timothy, and Cheryl Bostrom. *Children at Promise: 9 Principles to Help Kids Thrive in an At-Risk World.* San Francisco: Jossey-Bass, 2003.

Chapter 9. Who Chose to Give Kids So Many Choices?

Eisenberg, Arlene, Heidi Murkoff, and Sandee Hathaway. *What to Expect: The Toddler Years.* New York: Workman Publishing, 1994.

Farkas, Steve, Jean Johnson, and Ann Duffett. "A Lot Easier Said Than Done." Public Agenda Online, 2002.

Sears, William. *The Successful Child: What Parents Can Do to Help Kids Turn Out Well.* Boston: Little, Brown, 2002.

Swidey, Neil. "All Talked Out," *The Boston Globe Magazine,* November 7, 2004, 22–44.

Chapter 10. Feelings, Wo-oh-oh Feelings . . .

Easterbrook, Gregg. *The Progress Paradox.* New York: Random House, 2003.

Eisenberg, Arlene, Heidi Murkoff, and Sandee Hathaway, *What to Expect: The Toddler Years.* New York: Workman Publishing, 1994.

Farber, Adele, and Elaine Mazlish. *How to Talk So Kids Will Listen and Listen So Kids Will Talk.* New York: Quill, 1980.

Nelsen, Jane, Cheryl Erwin, and Carol Delzer. *Positive Discipline for Single Parents*. New York: Prima Publishing, 1999.

Schwartz, Jeffrey. *Brain Lock*. New York: ReganBooks, 1997.

———. *The Mind and the Brain: Neuroplasticity and the Power of Mental Force*. New York: ReganBooks, 2002.

Chapter 11. Led Zeppelin and the Culture Wars: The Culture Can Be Cool

Hersch, Patricia. *A Tribe Apart: A Journey into the Heart of American Adolescence*. New York: Ballantine Books, 1998.

Wallerstein, Judith, Julia Lewis, and Sandra Blakeslee. *The Unexpected Legacy of Divorce: A 25 Year Landmark Study*. New York: Hyperion, 2000.

Chapter 12. To Spank or Not to Spank (and Why It's Not Really the Right Question, Anyway)

Baumrind, D., R. E. Larzelere, and P. A. Cowan. "Ordinary Physical Punishment: Is It Harmful?" *Psychological Bulletin.*, vol. 128, 2002, 580–589.

Gershoff, Elizabeth. "Corporal Punishment by Parents and Associated Child Behaviors and Experiences: A Meta-Analytic and Theoretical Review." *Psychological Bulletin*, vol. 128, 2002, 539–579.

———. "Corporal Punishment, Physical Abuse and the Burden of Proof." *Psychological Bulletin*, vol. 128, 2002, pp. 602–611.

Gilbert, Susan. "Two Spanking Studies Indicate Parents Should Be Cautious." *The New York Times*, August 20, 1997, C8.

Hyman, Irwin. *The Case Against Spanking*. San Francisco: Jossey-Bass, 1997.

Kelly, Marguerite. *Marguerite Kelly's Family Almanac*. New York: Fireside, 1994.

Klass, Perri. "No More Yelling: The New Golden Rules of Discipline, from a Pediatrician Mom Who's Found Better Ways to Get Her Kids to Behave." *Parenting*, April 2004, 130–134.

Larzelere, Robert. "Child Outcomes of Nonabusive and Customary Physical Punishment by Parents: An Updated Literature Review." *Clinical Child and Family Psychology Review*, vol. 3, no. 4, 2000, 199–221.

———, et al. "Punishment Enhances Reasoning's Effectiveness as a Disciplinary Response to Toddlers." *Journal of Marriage and the Family*, vol. 60, 1998, 388–403.

Mulrine, Anna, and Rosellini, Lynn. "When to Spank." *U.S. News & World Report,* April 13, 1998, 52–58.

"A New Look at the Effects of Spanking." *The New York Times,* July 9, 2002, F8 (Associated Press).

Sears, William. *The Discipline Book: How to Have a Better Behaved Child from Birth to Age Ten.* Boston: Little, Brown, 1995.

Straus, Murray. *Beating the Devil Out of Them: Corporal Punishment in American Families.* Lanham, Md.: Lexington Books, 1994.

————, and V. E. Mouradian. "Impulsive Corporal Punishment by Mothers and Antisocial Behavior and Impulsiveness of Children." *Behavioral Sciences and the Law,* vol. 16, no. 3, 1998, 353–374.

————, D. B. Sugarman, and J. Giles-Sims. "Spanking by Parents and Subsequent Antisocial Behavior of Children." *Archives of Pediatrics and Adolescent Medicine,* vol. 151, 1997, 761–767.

Vedantam, Shankar. "Harm Outweighs Benefits of Spanking." *The Washington Post,* June 26, 2002.

Chapter 13. Challenge the Experts for the Sake of Your Child

Hulbert, Ann. *Raising America: Experts, Parents, and a Century of Advice About Children,* New York: Alfred A. Knopf, 2003.

Index

About the Author

BETSY HART'S nationally syndicated column, "From the Heart," offers practical views on cultural, family, and political issues and is distributed each week to newspapers across the country by the Scripps Howard News Service. Hart, also a popular television news commentator, is raising her young children—while contending with the parenting culture—in the Chicago area. Visit www.betsyhart.net.